# BIG ENGLISH ③

T0345719

## Contents

# unit 1 Wake Up!

 **1** **What's missing in the pictures? Match and write.**

do   eat   play

**1**

a  She _____ in the morning.

**2**

b  She _____ in the afternoon.

**3**

c  She _____ after school.

**2** **Read and circle.**

1  wake **up** / **off**          2  go **home** / **to home**

3  go to **park** / **the park**          4  go **school** / **to school**

5  **get** / **go** dressed          6  **watch** / **see** TV

**1:06**

## 3 Listen and write. Then match.

### Hurry, Kate!

a

It's Monday, ¹____.
Kate has to wake up.
Her mum sees the clock and says
Wake up sleepy head.

**Go, go, go! Hurry, Kate!**
**Hurry, Kate! You can't be late!**

Kate eats breakfast, she gets dressed.
It's ²____.
It's time to go to school.
And she can't be late!

**Chorus**

Kate's got her backpack
And she's got her lunch.
What time is it now?
Oh, no, it's time to go!

**Chorus**

b

## 4 Find out. Answer and draw. When does your friend wake up?

_____

_____

## 5 Read and circle.

**1** seven o'clock     **a** 7:00    **b** 6:00

**2** five twenty-five     **a** 2:25    **b** 5:25

**3** four forty-five     **a** 4:05    **b** 4:45

**4** two thirty     **a** 2:30    **b** 2:13

**6** **Read. Write T for true or F for false.**

**I Love Mondays!**

It's Monday and Luke wakes up. He says "Hooray! I love Mondays!" On Mondays, he's got Art at 11:10 before lunch. After lunch, at 2:15, he's got English. After school, he plays football or basketball. Luke eats breakfast and gets dressed. He puts on his shoes. He's ready for school but today there's no school. It's a holiday!

**1** Today is Monday. _____    **2** Luke has got Art after school. _____

**3** He's got English before lunch. _____    **4** He's ready for school. _____

**5** He plays football after school. _____    **6** He goes to school today. _____

**7** **Write about you. What do you do before school and after school?**

**1** Before school, _____.

**2** After school, _____.

THINK BIG

**What does Luke do next? Draw and write.**

Luke _____

_____

_____.

**8** Listen and stick. Number the pictures and answer.

a

When does she go to bed?

_____

b

When does she go to school?

_____

c

When does she eat breakfast?

_____

d

When does she wake up?

_____

**9** Correct the sentences for you.

**1** I do my homework in the morning.

_____

**2** I eat breakfast at 9:30.

_____

**3** I go home at 4:45.

_____

**4** I play basketball after school.

_____

**5** I watch TV in the morning, afternoon and evening.

_____

**10** **Read. Then write before or after.**

wakes up          eats breakfast          gets dressed          goes to school

does homework          watches TV          goes to bed

**1** Susan eats breakfast _____ she wakes up.

**2** She wakes up _____ she gets dressed.

**3** She gets dressed _____ she goes to school.

**4** She does her homework _____ she goes to school.

**5** She does her homework _____ she watches TV.

**6** She goes to bed _____ she does her homework.

**11** **Write the answers.**

**1** What does your brother or sister do before school?

_____

**2** What does your brother or sister do after school?

_____

**3** What does your mum or dad do before school?

_____

**4** What does your mum or dad do after school?

_____

**12** **Read and circle. Then number.**

**1** Wash your hands.

Our hands pick up germs that can make us **healthy / ill**.

Wash your hands after you cough or **sneeze / shower**.

**2** Have a shower.

Use warm water and soap to wash away **ill / bacteria**.

These are tiny living things that can make you **ill / dirty**.

**3** Brush your teeth.

Brush your teeth to keep them strong and **healthy / germs**.

Brushing your teeth stops tooth **clean / decay**.

a

b

c

**13** **Look and complete the chart.**

bath    face    hands    hair    shower    teeth

| have/take a | wash your | brush your | brush/comb your |
|---|---|---|---|
|  |  |  |  |
|  |  |  |  |

**THINK BIG** **Where can you find germs? Tick (✓) or cross (✗).**

☐ In the bathroom    ☐ In the garden    ☐ In the park

**14** Look at the times. Complete.

New York

Manuel

Texas

Maria

Montana

John

California

Kara

**1** It's one fifteen in New York. What time is it in Texas?  _____

**2** It's eleven fifteen in Montana. What time is it in Califormia?  _____

**3** It's ten fifteen. Where am I?  _____

**4** It's twelve fifteen. Where am I?  _____

**15** Read and answer.

**1** It's nine fifteen in California. What time is it in New York?  _____

**2** It's five fifteen in New York. What time is it in Montana?  _____

**3** In London, it's nine o'clock in the morning now and in Istanbul it's eleven in the morning. If it's eight fifteen in the morning in London, what time is it in Istanbul?  _____

**4** It's seven thirty in the evening in Paris and it's seven thirty in Cairo, too. If it's ten fifty at night in Paris, what time is it in Cairo?  _____

**16** **How many subjects and how many verbs can you find?**

Julie wakes up at 6:45. Then she eats breakfast. She washes her face. She brushes her teeth. She gets dressed. She goes to school at 8:30.

**17** **Underline the subject.**

**1** Jeff wakes up at 6:45 in the morning.

**2** We go to school at 7:30 in the morning.

**3** I feed my cat before school.

**4** Carol does the dishes in the evening.

**5** He plays basketball in the afternoon.

**18** **Underline the verb.**

**1** I make my bed before school.

**2** He rides his bike to school.

**3** They play video games after school.

**4** My sister reads books every day.

**5** My sister comes home at 3:45.

**19** **Write about three family members. What do they do?**

**Family Members**

| | | | |
|---|---|---|---|
| My aunt | My brother | My cousin | My father |
| My mother | My sister | My uncle | |

**1** _____ in the morning.

**2** _____ in the afternoon.

**3** _____ in the evening.

**20** **Read and circle a_e, i_e and o_e.**

face

bone

sheep

time

bike

soup

cake

note

**21** **Underline the words with a_e, i_e and o_e. Then read aloud.**

**1** The girl is eating a cake and the dog is eating a bone.

**2** I love my bike and my board game.

**22** **Connect the letters. Then write.**

**1** f            one    **a** _ _ _ _

**2** l            ace    **b** _ _ _ _

**3** b           ike     **c** _ _ _ _

1:18

**23** **Listen and write.**

What time is it?

It's time to play a ¹_____.

What time is it?

It's time to eat ²_____.

What time is it?

It's time to ride a ³_____.

What time is it?

It's time to go ⁴_____.

**24** **Match and write sentences for you. Use before or after.**

1 wash my     a a shower     _____

2 wash        b my teeth     _____

3 take        c face         _____

4 brush       d hair         _____

5 comb my     e my hands     _____

**25** **Put the words in order. Find out and then answer.**

1 | does | When | wake | your cousin | up? |

_____

_____

2 | When | her hands? | does | wash | your mum |

_____

_____

3 | bed? | your parents | When | go to | do |

_____

_____

4 | it | What | is | time | now? |

_____

_____

5 | you do | after school | What | do | on Fridays? |

_____

_____

# Lots of Jobs!

**1** Follow the paths and write the jobs.

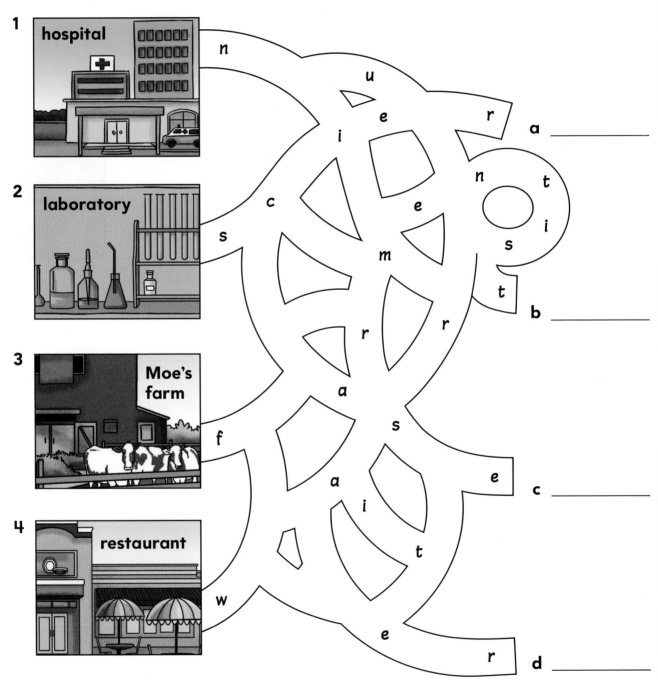

1 hospital

2 laboratory

3 Moe's farm

4 restaurant

a _____

b _____

c _____

d _____

**2** **Listen and number in order from 1–5. Then circle all the jobs.**

## Working Together

Working together, working hard.
Nurse, farmer, teacher and chef.

☐

Where does he work?
What does he do?
He's a firefighter
And he's very brave, too.

☐

There are many people
In our community.
So many jobs to do,
So many places to be.

☐

Where does she work?
What does she do?
She's a nurse.
And she always helps you.

☐

☐

Working together, working hard.
Nurse, farmer, teacher and chef.

**3** **Read and circle T for true or F for false.**

| | | | |
|---|---|---|---|
| 1 | A firefighter works on a farm. | T | F |
| 2 | A waiter works at a restaurant. | T | F |
| 3 | A police officer works at a shop. | T | F |
| 4 | A student studies at a university. | T | F |
| 5 | A cashier works at a laboratory. | T | F |

**4** **Choose a job and draw. Then answer.**

What does he/she do?

_____

_____

Where does he/she work?

_____

_____

**5** **Read. Then circle.**

**Is She a Doctor?**

Luke and his dad are at the hospital. They are looking for Luke's mum. Luke's mum works at the hospital. But she isn't a doctor. She's a cashier. She works in the hospital gift shop. Today's her birthday!

**1** Luke is looking for **a nurse** / **his mum**.

**2** Luke's mum works at the **post office** / **hospital**.

**3** Luke's mum is a **doctor** / **cashier**.

**4** She works in the **gift shop** / **supermarket**.

**6** **Answer the questions about a family member.**

**1** What does he or she do? _____

**2** Where does he or she work? _____

**THINK BIG**

How does Luke's mum celebrate her birthday? What does she do? Draw and write.

_____

_____

_____

**1:26**

**7** **Listen and stick. Then number.**

**a**

☐

**b**

☐

**c**

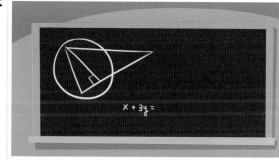

☐

**8** **Look and complete.**

1  **A:** What ¹_____ your brothers ²_____?
   **B:** They ³_____ firefighters.

   **A:** Where ⁴_____ they work?
   **B:** They ⁵_____ at the ⁶_____.

2  **A:** What ¹_____ your dad ²_____?
   **B:** He ³_____ a waiter.

   **A:** Where ⁴_____ he ⁵_____?
   **B:** He ⁶_____ at a Spanish ⁷_____.

1:28

**9** 🎧 **Listen and ✓.**

**1** What does Peggy's dad do?

He's ☐ a cashier.  ☐ a teacher.  ☐ a farmer.

**2** Where does Peggy's mum work?

She works ☐ at a restaurant.  ☐ at a police station.  ☐ at a fire station.

**3** Where does Peggy's brother work?

He works ☐ at a laboratory.  ☐ at a university.  ☐ at a school.

**4** What does her sister do?

She's ☐ a chef.  ☐ a student.  ☐ a police officer.

**10** **Read. Write Where or What.**

**1 A:** _____ does your brother work?
   **B:** He works at a post office.

**2 A:** _____ does your sister do?
   **B:** She's a nurse.

**3 A:** _____ do you do?
   **B:** I'm a scientist.

**4 A:** _____ do your parents work?
   **B:** They work on a farm.

**11** **Put the words in order.**

**1** | does | uncle | What | do? | your |

_____

**2** | waiter. | He's | a |

_____

**3** | at | He | a | works | restaurant. |

_____

**12** **Read and match.**

1 Susie is a fashion designer.

2 Jake is an artist.

3 Mark is a photographer.

a   b   c

**13** **Complete the crossword. Use the clues and the words in the box.**

designer   gallery   landscapes   photographer   sketch   upload

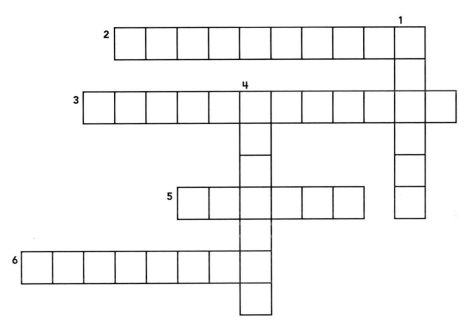

**Down ↓**

1 When Susie's got an idea she draws a ❓ .

4 Jake shows his paintings in an art ❓ .

**Across →**

2 Jake likes painting the mountains. He paints ❓ .

3 A ❓ takes photos of people and places.

5 I ❓ my photos to the computer.

6 Susie loves drawing clothes. She's a fashion ❓ .

**When Susie sees people wearing her clothes, she feels excited. When do you feel excited?**

When I _____ , I feel excited.

**14** **Read. Find the three countries.**

Lalana lives in Thailand. She helps schools. Lalana and her friends ask people for books. They give the books to schools.

Marcus lives in Australia. Marcus and his friends clean up the streets. They pick up rubbish before school.

Carla lives in Spain. Carla and her big sister help tourists. Tourists visit Spain. They get lost. Carla and her big sister find the places they are looking for.

**15** **Look at 14. Write.**

books     rubbish     tourists

**1** Carla and her sister help _____ who are lost.

**2** Marcus and his friends pick up the _____ on the streets.

**3** Lalana and her friends give _____ to schools.

**16** **Can you help your community? What can you do? Write and draw.**

I can help _____

_____

_____

_____

_____

**17** **Circle the subjects and underline the verbs.**

Steve and Mohammed are friends. They work at a laboratory. They play basketball and watch TV on a Saturday.

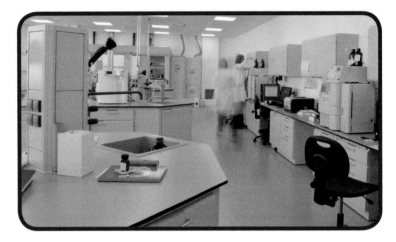

**18** **Rachel and Kate are sisters. Read and complete.**

**Rachel**
I am a police officer.
I dance.
I sing.
I live on a farm.

**Kate**
I am a teacher.
I dance.
I play the piano.
I live in a city.

1 _____ and _____ are sisters.

2 _____ and _____ dance.

3 _____ dances and sings.

4 _____ dances and plays the piano.

5 _____ lives in a city.

6 _____ lives on a farm.

**19** **Write about you.**

I _____ and _____ in the evening.

My friend and I _____ after school.

**20** **Read and circle sm, st, sk and sp.**

smile

game

spoon

storm

space

smart

ski star skate

note

**21** **Underline the words with sm, st, sk and sp. Then read aloud.**

**1** There are small stars in space.

**2** We skate and ski in winter.

**22** **Connect the letters. Then write.**

**1** sm          oon   **a** _ _ _ _ _

**2** sp           ar    **b** _ _ _ _

**3** st           i     **c** _ _ _

**4** sk           ile   **d** _ _ _ _ _

1:36

**23** **Listen and write.**

¹ _____ and look.
Look at the ² _____,
The stars in ³ _____,
And ⁴ _____!

**24** **Look and complete. Then answer.**

**1** What _____ your sister do?

☐ **a** She's a teacher.
☐ **b** She's a police officer.

**2** What _____ your mum _____?

☐ **a** She's a waiter.
☐ **b** She's a scientist.

**3** What _____ your brothers do?

☐ **a** They're firefighters.
☐ **b** They're students.

**4** What _____ your cousins _____?

☐ **a** They're nurses.
☐ **b** They're farmers.

**25** **Read and match.**

**1** I like dancing. When I

**2** When they take a photo, they

**3** When she's got an idea,

**4** When he sees a beautiful landscape,

**5** I get ideas when

**a** she draws a sketch.

**b** dance, I feel happy.

**c** he paints it.

**d** I go to an art gallery.

**e** upload it to a computer.

# unit 3

# Working Hard!

**1** **Follow and write. Use the words in the box.**

bed    dog    dishes    fish
piano    room    rubbish    test

1 clean — my

2 do — the

3 feed — the

4 make — my

5 practise — the

6 study — for — a

7 take — out — the

8 walk — the

_____

_____

_____

_____

_____

_____

_____

_____

1:40

**2** **Listen. What things do they do? Match. Then write.**

1 Tara _____
_____ .

2 Dave _____
_____ .

3 Christy _____
_____ .

4 Matt _____
_____ .

a

b

c

d

**3** Listen and circle.

### Different Twins

My name's Matt
And my name's Mike.
We want to talk to you.
I do my chores
And I do, too.
But we are not alike.

**Mike and Matt, Matt and Mike.**
**These two twins are not alike.**

I'm Matt,
I always **take out the rubbish / clean my room.**
I do my chores each day.
I sometimes **do the dishes / study for a test**
And then we go and play.

**Chorus**

I'm Mike,
I always **clean my room / make my bed.**
I do my chores each day.
I sometimes **feed the fish / walk the dog**
And then we go and play.

**Chorus**

**4** What chores do you do? Write four sentences.

_____

_____

_____

_____

**5** Read. Then number in order.

Amy is thinking. She's making a list. She has to do lots of things before school. She has to eat breakfast. She has to brush her teeth. Then she has to feed her fish, clean her room and study for her Maths test. Amy goes to school at 7:50. Her alarm clock says 7:05. Mum says "It's 7:45." Amy's clock isn't working! She has to get a new alarm clock.

_____ She has to study for her Maths test.

_____ She has to feed the fish.

_____ She has to brush her teeth.

_____ Amy has to eat breakfast.

_____ She has to get a new alarm clock.

_____ She has to clean her room.

**6** Write. What do you have to do before school?

I have to _____ before school.

**Think and write for you.**

**THINK BIG**

**1** I have to _____ before I go to bed.

**2** I have to _____ before I go to bed.

**3** I have to _____ before I go to bed.

**4** I have to _____ before I go to bed.

1:46

**7** Listen and stick.

| Monday | Tuesday | Wednesday | Thursday | Friday |
|--------|---------|-----------|----------|--------|
|        |         |           |          |        |

**8** Read and circle the correct words.

**1 A:** What **do** / **does** Nancy have to do after school?

**B:** She **have to** / **has to** practise the piano.

**2 A:** What **do** / **does** we have to do this evening?

**B:** We **have to** / **has to** study for our test tomorrow.

**3 A:** What **do** / **does** you have to do every morning?

**B:** I **have to** / **has to** make my bed.

**9** What do they have to do? Look and write.

Kate and Ted                    Jane                    Jim and Mike

**1** Kate: _____

**2** Ted: _____

**3** Jane: _____

**4** Jim and Mike: _____

# Language in Action

**10** **Look and match.**

**1** always

| | Sun | Mon | Tue | Wed | Thurs | Fri | Sat |
|---|---|---|---|---|---|---|---|
| **a** | | | | | | | |

**2** usually

| | Sun | Mon | Tue | Wed | Thurs | Fri | Sat |
|---|---|---|---|---|---|---|---|
| **b** | | | | | | | |

**3** sometimes

| | Sun | Mon | Tue | Wed | Thurs | Fri | Sat |
|---|---|---|---|---|---|---|---|
| **c** | | | | | | | |

**4** never

| | Sun | Mon | Tue | Wed | Thurs | Fri | Sat |
|---|---|---|---|---|---|---|---|
| **d** | | | | | | | |

**11** **Complete with always, usually, sometimes or never.**

**1** I _____ feed the fish.

**2** I _____ study for tests.

**3** I _____ take out the rubbish.

**4** I _____ do the dishes.

| | M | T | W | T | F |
|---|---|---|---|---|---|
| feed the fish | ✔ | | ✔ | | ✔ |
| study for a test | | | | ✔ | ✔ |
| take out the rubbish | | | | | |
| do the dishes | ✔ | ✔ | ✔ | ✔ | ✔ |

**12** **Complete for you. Use the verbs in the box.**

clean    do    make    practise    study    take

**1** I usually _____.

**2** I sometimes _____.

**3** I never _____.

**4** I always _____.

**13** **Read and complete the charts. Then write.**

Sam and Becca do chores. Their parents give them pocket money every Friday. Pocket money is money they earn when they do their chores. Sam wants to earn €5 this week. Becca wants to earn €6 this week.

| Sam's chores | Amount (in euros) | Number of Times | Subtotal (in euros) |
|---|---|---|---|
| do the dishes | 50c | 3 | €1.50 |
| walk the dog | €1 | | |
| make his bed | 25c | | €1.50 |
| | | | €5 |

How many times does Sam have to walk the dog? _____

| Becca's chores | Amount (in euros) | Number of Times | Subtotal (in euros) |
|---|---|---|---|
| do the dishes | 50c | 4 | €2 |
| help cook dinner | €1 | 3 | |
| make her bed | 25c | | €1 |
| | | | €6 |

How many times does Becca have to make her bed? _____

I earn two euros each time I clean my room. I clean it twice a week. How much pocket money do I earn?

**THINK BIG** **Read and ✓.**

€2 x 1 = €2 ☐   €2 x 2 = €4 ☐   €1 x 3 = €3 ☐

**Read. Then circle the chores.**

**1** Leah lives in Alaska. In winter, it snows a lot. Leah has to shovel snow before school.

**2** Ivan lives on a goat farm. His family makes goat cheese. Ivan has to get up at 5 o'clock in the morning to help his dad. He feeds the goats and gets the milk before school.

**3** Chen Wei lives in Singapore. Her mother has got a noodle shop. In the evening, Chen Wei does her homework. Then she has to help her mother make noodles.

**15** **Look at 14 and answer.**

**1** What does Leah have to do before school?

_____

**2** Who does Ivan have to help?

_____

**3** What does Ivan have to do?

_____

**4** Who does Chen Wei have to help?

_____

**5** What does Chen Wei have to make?

_____

**THINK BIG** **Tick (✓) the chores.**

go to a party ☐          clean the kitchen ☐

play in the garden ☐          feed the fish ☐

**16** **Read. Then ✗ the words we don't write in capitals.**

> Use **capital letters** for most words in titles.
> **I H**ave a **L**ot to **D**o!
>
> But always use capital letters for the first word in a title.
> **A** Day at the Park with Grandma

and, but, or, a, an, the ☐

grandpa, mum, brother ☐

at, for, in, on, to, with ☐

big, good ☐

help, walk, eat ☐

Taking Care of a Big Dog

Good Things to Eat

My Brother and I

**17** **Circle the title with the correct capitals.**

**1** A big blue balloon
a Big Blue Balloon
A Big Blue Balloon

**2** The Chef and the Waiter
the Chef and the Waiter
The Chef And The Waiter

**3** Harry Needs a Helping Hand
Harry needs a Helping Hand
Harry Needs A Helping Hand

**4** Dinner At Grandpa's House
Dinner at Grandpa's House
Dinner at grandpa's house

**18** **Write the correct title. Use capital letters.**

1 _____

uncle Joe's dream
penguin trouble at the zoo
a surprise for grandma

2 _____

3 _____

**19** **Read and circle ay and oy.**

bike    say    day

May    boy

toy    stop    joy

**20** **Underline the words with ay and oy. Then read aloud.**

**1** On Sundays we play all day with our toys.

**2** I'm reading the story of a boy called Roy.

**21** **Connect the letters. Then write.**

**1** d                    oy    **a** _ _ _

**2** t                    ay    **b** _ _ _

1:55

**22** **Listen and write.**

What do we ¹ _____?
It's May, it's ² _____,
It's a nice ³ _____.
Come on, girls!
Come on, ⁴ _____!
Bring your ⁵ _____.

**23** **Look, read and ✓.**

I clean my room three times a week. I get fifty cents each time. How much pocket money do I earn?

I take out the rubbish four times a week. I get one euro each time. How much pocket money do I earn?

50c x 2 = €1 ☐

€3 x 1= €3 ☐

50c x 3 = €1.50 ☐

€1 x 3= €3 ☐

€1 x 4= €4 ☐

50c x 3 = €1.50 ☐

**24** **Look. Write T for true or F for false.**

| Alicia's Chores | Monday | Tuesday | Wednesday | Thursday | Friday |
|---|---|---|---|---|---|
| make the bed | ✓ | ✓ | ✓ | ✓ | ✓ |
| do the dishes | ✓ | | ✓ | | |
| feed the fish | ✓ | ✓ | ✓ | ✓ | |
| take out the rubbish | | | | | |

**1** Alicia always makes the bed. _____

**2** Alicia never does the dishes. _____

**3** Alicia usually feeds the fish. _____

**4** Alicia sometimes takes out the rubbish. _____

**25** **Look and write about Josh and Adam. Use has to and have to.**

**1** Josh and Adam _____

_____ dog.

**2** _____

_____ piano.

| | Josh | Adam |
|---|---|---|
| walk the dog | ✓ | ✓ |
| practise the piano | ✓ | |
| study for a test | ✓ | ✓ |
| clean his room | | ✓ |

**3** _____ test.

**4** _____ room.

# Sue's Busy Day

**1** Choose one path. Draw the path. Learn about Sue's busy day.

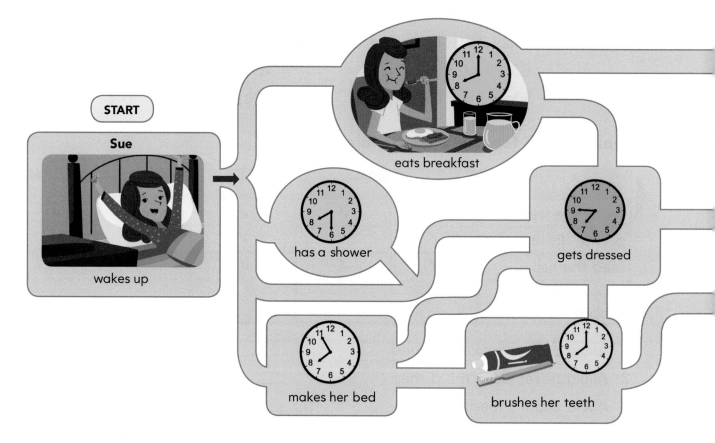

START

Sue

wakes up

eats breakfast

has a shower

gets dressed

makes her bed

brushes her teeth

**2** Look at your path in 1. Guess and write.

**1** What time does Sue wake up? She wakes up at _____.

**2** What does Sue do? She's a _____.

**3** Look at your path in 1. Write five sentences about Sue's day.

**1** _____

**2** _____

**3** _____

**4** _____

**5** _____

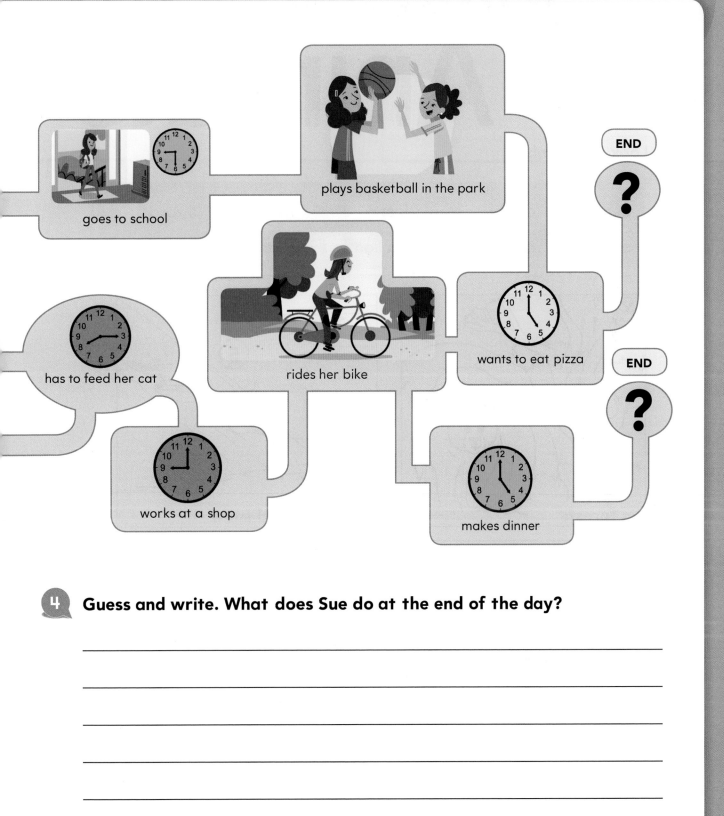

**4** **Guess and write. What does Sue do at the end of the day?**

_____

_____

_____

_____

_____

_____

unit 4

# Amazing Animals

## 1 Look and number.

| | | | | |
|---|---|---|---|---|
| bear ☐ | camel ☐ | deer ☐ | fish ☐ | lizard ☐ |
| owl ☐ | penguin ☐ | sea lion ☐ | shark ☐ | snake ☐ |

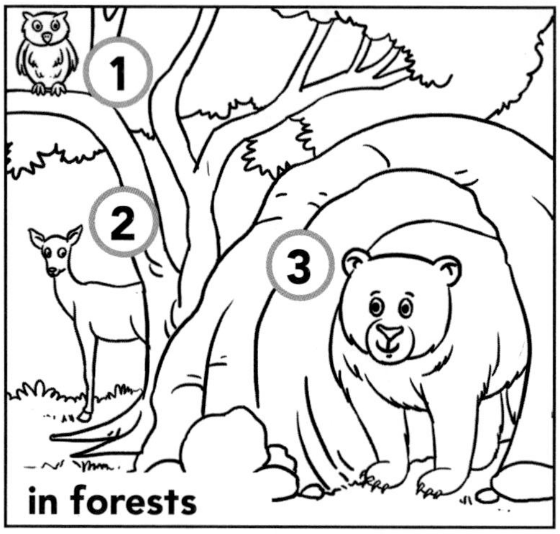

in forests

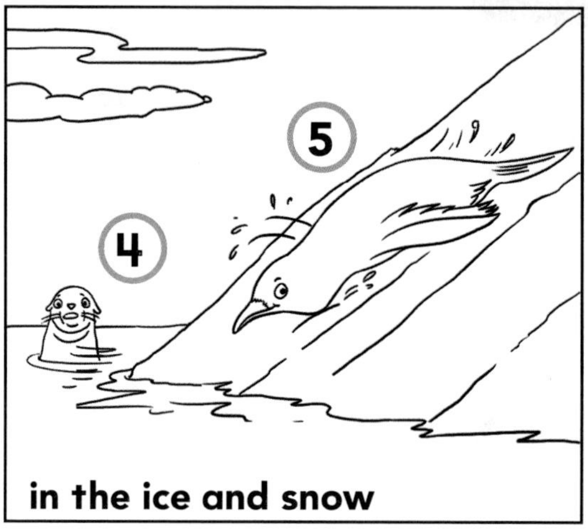

in the ice and snow

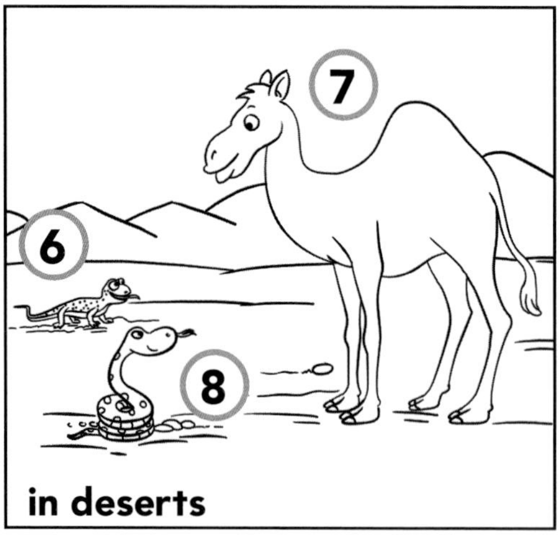

in deserts

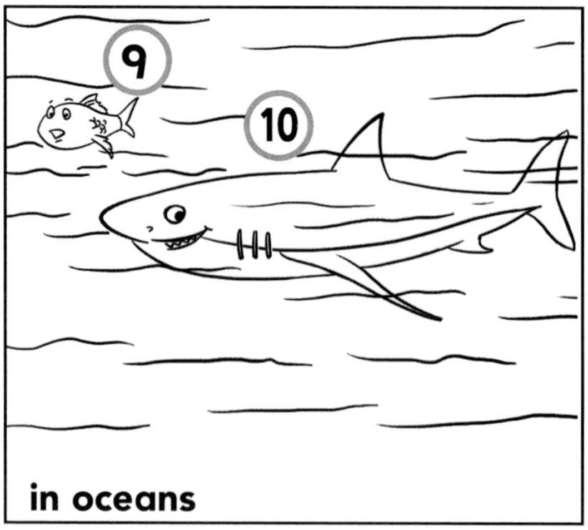

in oceans

## 2 Write.

My favourite animals are ______________________________.

They ______________________________________________.

**3** **Listen and write. Then number. Underline the places.**

a

☐

c

☐

e

☐

## Animals Are Amazing!

Animals are amazing!
We see them far and near.
Some live in forests
Like ¹ _____, ² _____
and ³ _____.
Some live in deserts
Like ⁴ _____
and some ⁵ _____.
Some live in water,
In oceans, seas and lakes.

**Amazing, amazing animals
What can animals do?
They can fly, they can swim, they can jump!
We share the earth with you!**

b

☐

d

☐

**4** **Answer the questions.**

1 Where do bears live?

_____

2 Where do fish live?

_____

3 Where do toucans live?

_____

4 Where do camels live?

_____

# Story

**5** **Read. Then write can or can't.**

## At the Zoo

Luke and Amy are at the zoo. They watch a sea lion show. The sea lion can clap to music. It can't sing very well so Luke covers his ears. The sea lion can balance a ball. It can do lots of tricks. Luke and Amy go to the parrot show. The parrot can ride a bike. It can say its name. It can talk! The parrot can't stop talking.

**1** The sea lion _____ clap to music.

**2** The sea lion _____ sing well.

**3** The sea lion _____ do tricks.

**4** The parrot _____ ride a bike.

**5** The parrot _____ say its name.

**6** The parrot _____ stop talking.

**6** **Write about what you can do.**

| balance a ball on your nose    clap to music    ride a bike    sing well |

I can _____.

I can't _____.

**THINK BIG**

| do tricks   fly |
| jump   swim |
| talk   walk |

Sea lions can _____.

They can't _____.

Parrots _____.

_____

2:08

**7** Listen and stick. Then number.

**a**  **b** 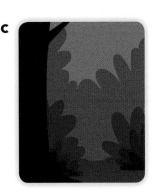 **c** **d**

☐     ☐     ☐     ☐

**8** Look and complete the sentences. Use **can** or **can't**.

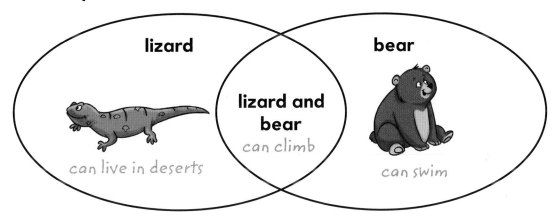

**lizard**     **lizard and bear** can climb     **bear**

can live in deserts        can swim

**1** Lizards and bears _____.

**2** Lizards _____ but bears _____.

**3** Bears _____ but lizards _____.

**9** Read and circle.

**1** Can **a camel / camels** live in deserts?
Yes, it can.

**2** Can **a lizard / lizards** climb? Yes, they can.

**3** Can **bears / a bear** fly? No, they can't.

**4** Can **a shark / sharks** walk? No, it can't.

## Language in Action

**10**　**Answer the questions.**

**1**　Can a bear climb?

_____

**2**　Can penguins fly?

_____

**3**　Can a shark sing?

_____

**4**　Can lizards talk?

_____

**5**　Can sea lions do tricks?

_____

**11**　**Look and complete. Use the words in the box.**

| can | can't | fly | swim | they |

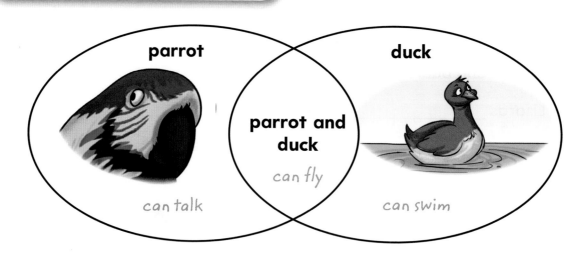

**parrot**

**parrot and duck**

_can fly_

**duck**

_can talk_

_can swim_

Parrots and ducks can ¹_____. Parrots ²_____ talk
but ³_____ can't swim. Ducks can ⁴_____ but they
⁵_____ talk.

**12** **Label the pictures. Then read and match.**

chameleon    grey tree frog    polar bear    stonefish

1 _____   2 _____   3 _____   4 _____

**a** It uses camouflage to hide. It looks like tree bark. _____

**b** It's got white fur so it's not easy to see in the snow. _____

**c** It looks like stones at the bottom of the sea. _____

**d** It can change its colour to blend into its surroundings. It can be green or brown. _____

**13** **Read and ✓.**

|  | stonefish | tree frog | chameleon | polar bear |
|---|---|---|---|---|
| **1** It can change colour. |  |  |  |  |
| **2** It lives in the snow. |  |  |  |  |
| **3** It looks like stones. |  |  |  |  |
| **4** It looks like a branch. |  |  |  |  |

**THINK BIG**

**Complete and colour.**

**1** A chameleon on a brown rock is _____.

**2** A chameleon on a green branch is _____.

**Match and complete.**

**1** My name is Graham. I live in England. I've got a _____. I like playing with it in the garden.

**a**

**2** I'm Maria. I live in Italy. I've got a _____. It's got soft fur. It's grey.

**b**

**3** My name is Laura. I live in Mexico. We've got a colourful _____. It can sing.

**c**

**4** My name is Cheng. I live in China. My family have got a _____ in a bowl. It's a popular pet here.

**d**

15 **Write about you. Complete the sentences.**

My name is _____. I live in _____.

_____ are popular pets here.

They can _____ and _____.

They can't _____ or _____.

**16** **Read. Circle the best topic sentence for the main idea.**

1 Main Idea: Polar bears are my favourite animal.

    **a** Polar bears live in cold places.

    **b** Some days are cold in the winter.

    **c** I like polar bears.

2 Main idea: It's important to take care of pets.

    **a** I want a pet parakeet.

    **b** I feed my cat every day.

    **c** People all over the world have got pets.

3 Main idea: Some animals can change colour.

    **a** Some animals can look like different things.

    **b** Some animals are not good pets.

    **c** Some animals can do tricks.

4 Main idea: Zoos are great places.

    **a** A parrot can talk.

    **b** I always have fun at the zoo.

    **c** Dogs are fun pets.

**17** **Write a topic sentence for the following titles.**

1 My Favourite Animal

_____

2 My Favourite Time of Day

_____

3 An Unusual Job

_____

**18** **Read and circle ea, oi and oe.**

> eat
>
> Spain
>
> boil
>
> bean
>
> meat
>
> toe
>
> oil
>
> joy

**19** **Underline the words with ea, oi and oe. Then read aloud.**

**1** Joe likes boiled beans with oil.

**2** I eat meat and drink tea.

**20** **Connect the letters. Then write.**

**1** p          oil          **a** _ _ _ _

**2** b          oe           **b** _ _ _

**3** t          each         **c** _ _ _ _ _

2:18

**21** **Listen and write.**

So, Joe, boil the ¹_____,

Add the ²_____,

Add the ³_____.

Eat the ⁴_____,

Eat the meat,

Eat the ⁵_____

And drink the ⁶_____.

**22** **Read and answer.**

1 Can snakes eat sharks? _____

2 Can a bear climb? _____

3 Can a lizard sing? _____

4 Can parrots talk? _____

**23** **Think about the animals you know. Complete the chart.**

| These animals can swim. | These animals can fly. | These animals can climb trees. |
|---|---|---|
| 1 | 1 | 1 |
| 2 | 2 | 2 |
| 3 | 3 | 3 |
| 4 | 4 | 4 |

**24** **Match the questions and answers.**

1 What can toucans do?

2 What can you do?

3 Can an owl jump?

4 Can a shark swim?

5 What can a parrot do?

6 Can deer jump and run?

a Yes, it can.

b They can fly.

c Yes, they can.

d No, it can't but it can fly.

e I can swim, run and talk.

f It can fly but it can't swim.

**25** **Correct the sentences.**

1 Sea lions and sharks can't swim. _____

2 Bears can't swim or climb trees. _____

3 Penguins live in lakes. _____

4 A camel can fly. _____

5 A chameleon can't change colour. _____

# unit 5 Wonderful Weather!

**1** **Match.**

**1**

**2**

**3**

**4**

**5**

**6**

 **a** It's hot and sunny.

**b** It's windy.

**c** It's cool and cloudy.

 **d** It's cold and snowy.

 **e** It's rainy.

 **f** It's warm.

**2** **What's the weather like today?**

It's _____.

It isn't _____.

**3** **Listen and circle the five incorrect words. Then listen and write.**

### Cool Weekend!

**What's the weather like today?**
**Rainy, windy, hot or cold?**

On Sunday, it was rainy,
It was very hot, too.
I was nice and cool in my winter coat,
Outside the sky wasn't blue!

Now, it's Tuesday. It's sunny.
Great! I can go out and play.
Oh, no! I have to go to school.
Never mind! The weekend was cold!

**Chorus (x2)**

1 _____

2 _____

3 _____

4 _____

5 _____

**4** **Look at 1. Complete the sentences. Use words from the box.**

coat   scarf   shorts   sunglasses   T-shirt

**1** On hot and sunny days, Jim wears _____.

**2** On warm days, Iris wears a _____.

**3** On cloudy and cool days, Dan wears a _____.

**4** On warm rainy days, Maria wears _____ and boots.

**5** On cold and snowy days, Joe wears a _____.

**5** **What was the weather like yesterday? Draw and write.**

It was _____. It wasn't _____.

**6** Read and ✓.

## Amy is Ready!

Amy is going on a hike. It was rainy yesterday. Amy's mum doesn't want her to get wet today so Amy gets a raincoat and an umbrella. It was cold and windy yesterday. Amy's mum doesn't want her to get cold so she gets her jumper, her hat and gloves. It's sunny today. Amy's mum gives her sunscreen and sunglasses. Now Amy's ready!

**1** It was rainy yesterday. Amy gets

☐ sunglasses.    ☐ an umbrella.    ☐ a jumper.    ☐ a raincoat.

**2** It was cold and windy yesterday. Amy gets

☐ a jumper.    ☐ sandals.    ☐ shorts.    ☐ gloves.

**3** It's warm and sunny now. Amy's mum gives her

☐ boots.    ☐ a coat.    ☐ sunscreen.    ☐ sunglasses.

**7** **Read and write.**

cloudy   cool   cold   hot   rainy   snowy

**1** What is the weather like today? It is _____.

**2** What was the weather like yesterday? It was _____.

**THINK BIG** Draw and write.

**HOT**

**COLD**

I wear _____ on sunny days.

I wear _____ on cold days.

2:27

**8** **Listen and stick.**

| San Francisco | |
|---|---|
| Yesterday | Today |
| | |

| Puerto Rico | |
|---|---|
| Yesterday | Today |
| | |

**9** **What was the weather like? Match and write.**

1  On Monday, _____ .

2  _____

3  _____

4  _____

5  _____

# Language in Action

**10** **Read and look. Circle T for true and F for false.**

| Yesterday | Today |
|-----------|-------|

| | | | |
|---|---|---|---|
| **1** | Yesterday, the weather was cool. | T | F |
| **2** | It wasn't windy yesterday. | T | F |
| **3** | It's cloudy today. | T | F |
| **4** | It's cold today. | T | F |
| **5** | It was sunny yesterday. | T | F |
| **6** | It's cool and sunny today. | T | F |

**11** **Look at 10. Write the answers.**

1 What was the weather like yesterday? _____

2 What is the weather like today? _____

**12** **Write about you.**

1 What was the weather like yesterday? _____

**13** **Read and make sentences.**

1 I / ✗ / hot / yesterday

_____

2 We / ✗ / cool / last weekend

_____

3 It / ✓ / sunny / now

_____

4 It / ✗ / windy / today

_____

**14** **Read and complete. Use the words in the box.**

| average | climate | extreme | opposite | temperature | tourists |

    The weather in a place is called the ¹_____. In the places in the photos, the climate is ²_____ – the weather is very hot, cold or rainy. It's very hot in the Lut Desert. The ³_____ can reach 70 degrees Celsius. The Atacama Desert in Chile looks like the moon. Lots of ⁴_____ visit it every year. This rainforest gets an ⁵_____ of 13 metres of rain each year. The climate in Oymyakon, Russia, is the ⁶_____ of the Lut Desert. It isn't hot, it's very cold.

**15** **Read and match.**

1  Not many people go to the Lut Desert.
2  The Atacama desert is very dry
3  It rains a lot in Lloró, Colombia.
4  Not many people live in Oymakyon

a  because of the cold climate.
b  As a result, the trees grow quickly.
c  As a result, it's a quiet place.
d  because it never rains.

**Find the odd one out.**

THINK
BIG

1  Lloró
3  Lut Desert

2  Atacama Desert
4  Oymyakon, Russia

The odd one out is _____

because _____.

**16** **Read. Then circle the weather words.**

Children around the world like to play sports in all kinds of weather.

On windy days, some children fly kites in Japan.

On rainy days, some children in Africa go swimming and play games in the water.

On cold and snowy days, some children go dog sledging in Alaska.

**17** **Match the sentences.**

1 Some children fly kites
2 Some children in Africa go swimming
3 Some children go dog sledging

a on rainy days.
b on cold and snowy days.
c on windy days.

**18** **Do you like these sports? Write numbers to rate them.**

> 1 = I love it!     2 = I like it.     3 = I don't like it.

_____ flying kites          _____ riding a bike          _____ playing volleyball
_____ swimming          _____ doing gymnastics          _____ playing football
_____ sledging          _____ running          _____ playing baseball

**19** **Read. Number the detail sentences 1 or 2 to go with topic sentence 1 or 2.**

Topic sentence 1: *I like hot, sunny weather.*

Topic sentence 2: *My best friend is Julie.*

☐

**a** I swim in the sea on hot days.

☐

**b** Julie is in my class at school.

☐

**c** She wants to be a firefighter.

☐

**d** We play football together after school.

☐

**e** I like riding my bike in the sun.

☐

**f** I want to go to a desert.

**20** **Write the best detail sentence to start each paragraph. Choose from the box.**

Cats were everywhere!   I take care of my pet every day.   Maths is fun.

**1** Topic sentence: I've got a pet.

Detail sentences: My pet's name is Tiny. He is a very small fish. He loves swimming every day.

_____

_____

**2** Topic sentence: Maths is my favourite subject.

Detail sentences: Maths is easy for me. I help my friends with it.

_____

_____

**21** **Read and circle sc, sw, sn and sl.**

snail    snow                    scout

coin            slow

sweet                            foe

swim        sleep

scarf

**22** **Underline the words with sc, sw, sn and sl. Then read aloud.**

**1** There is a swan sleeping on the swing.

**2** Put on your scarf and put on your skiis. It's snowing!

**23** **Connect the letters. Then write.**

**1** sl          ail      **a** _ _ _ _ _

**2** sn         arf      **b** _ _ _ _ _

**3** sw        eep      **c** _ _ _ _ _

**4** sc         eet      **d** _ _ _ _ _

2:35

**24** **Listen and write.**

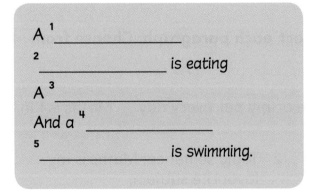

A ¹ _____

² _____ is eating

A ³ _____

And a ⁴ _____

⁵ _____ is swimming.

**25** **Read and choose.**

1 It's hot and dry there **because** / **so** it never rains.

2 **As** / **So** a result, few people live there.

3 The trees grow quickly because **of** / **to** the rainy climate.

4 **No** / **Not** many trees grow there because it's so hot.

5 Not many people live there **because of** / **few** the extreme temperature.

**26** **Read and complete with is, isn't, was, wasn't.**

**Emily:** Hi, Sam. It ¹_____ fun to see you yesterday.

**Sam:** Yes, I had fun, too.

**Emily:** What ²_____ the weather like this afternoon?

**Sam:** It was cool this morning but it ³_____ hot now.

**Emily:** It's the same here! It ⁴_____ hot this morning but it is hot now.

**Sam:** That's funny. I am happy it ⁵_____ rainy. I don't like the rain.

**Emily:** I love the rain. I can watch TV!

# Smells Good!

 **1** **Complete the sentences. Use words from the box.**

| feels | looks | smell | sounds | tastes |

**1** My jumper _____ soft.

**2** This pie _____ delicious.

**3** This music _____ amazing.

**4** My hair _____ terrible.

**5** These flowers _____ nice.

**2** **Write about you.**

**1** What smells awful? _____

**2** What smells wonderful? _____

**3** Listen and number in order.

2:40

### Grandma's House

We always do my favourite thing
Baking ginger cookies.
They taste so nice and yummy,
We are both very lucky! ☐

**Yummy smells and her smiling face.**
**We really love my Grandma's place.** ☐

We love my Grandma's house.
It always smells so nice.
It smells like ginger cookies
Sweet, with a little spice! ☐

Grandma likes playing old songs
From when she was very young.
The music sounds so wonderful,
We have to sing along. ☐

**Chorus** ☐

**4** Look and read. Then circle.

**1** How does the apple taste? It tastes **delicious** / **bad**.

**2** How do these shoes feel? They feel **soft** / **tight**.

**3** How does my hair look? It looks **terrible** / **nice**.

**4** How does the band sound? The band sounds **bad** / **good**.

**5** How do the flowers smell? They smell **awful** / **sweet**.

# Story

**5** **Look and read. Then write Luke or Amy.**

**It Tastes Terrible!**

Luke smells the fish soup. He thinks it smells horrible. He thinks the soup looks bad, too. Amy tastes the soup and says, "It tastes... OK." Luke tries the soup. He says, "It tastes terrible." Amy has got a cold. She can't smell or taste the soup.

**1** _____ thinks the soup smells bad.　　**2** _____ thinks the soup doesn't look good.

**3** _____ thinks the soup tastes OK.　　**4** _____ thinks the soup tastes terrible.

**5** _____ can't taste or smell the soup.

**6** **Think and write about you. Use smell or taste and the words from the box or your own ideas.**

I think _____ terrible.

I think _____ nice.

I think _____ horrible.

I think _____ delicious.

a clean sock
a flower   chocolate
fish soup   ice cream

**THINK BIG** **Put in order.**

awful   great   good   bad   OK

_____ very bad _____ _____ _____ very good _____

2:44

**7** Listen and stick. Then number.

a  ☐

b  ☐

c  ☐

d  ☐

**8** Read and circle. Then complete. Use the words from the box.

> delicious    nice    quiet    soft    tight

**1** I'm wearing my new shoes.

They **taste / feel** _____.

**2** My baby brother isn't crying.

The house **tastes / sounds** _____.

**3** I'm taking a walk in the garden.

The flowers **smell / sound** _____.

**4** I'm eating my favourite lunch.

It **feels / tastes** _____.

**5** You're wearing my new jumper.

It **looks / sounds** _____.

**9** **Circle the correct word.**

1 How **do** / **does** the soup taste?  2 How **do** / **does** the pizza taste?

3 How **do** / **does** the sandals feel?  4 How **do** / **does** the apples smell?

5 How **do** / **does** the music sound?  6 How **do** / **does** the shirts look?

**10** **Complete the questions. Then look and complete the answers.**

1 **A:** How _____ the sand feel?  2 **A:** How _____ the hat look?

  **B:** It _____ hot.      **B:** It _____ pretty.

3 **A:** How _____ the birds   4 **A:** How _____ the sandwiches
   sound?              taste?

  **B:** They _____ loud.     **B:** They _____ delicious.

**11** **Draw an interesting or funny cake. Colour. Then write.**

1 How does it taste?

_____

2 How does it smell?

_____

3 How does it look?

_____

**12** **Find the words and write.**

ensak

1 _____

haleoncem

2 _____

yutbferlt

3 _____

tab

4 _____

**13** **Read and circle.**

Animals and people have got senses. Our senses take in **smell / information** about the world. They send this to our **brain / tongue**. We use our senses to **understand / avoid** the world around us. Our senses keep us safe and help us to avoid **danger / food**. Some animals' senses are different from people's senses. For example, bats use their ears to 'see'. They make a sound, then listen for the **music / echo**.

**THINK BIG**

**Which animals use these senses? Match.**

a
shark

b
elephant

c
tarsier

1 Because of its large ears, it's got a very good sense of hearing. It also uses its trunk and feet to hear.

2 It uses its big eyes to find food at night.

3 It's got a good sense of smell. It can smell food in the water from far away.

**14** **Read and circle all the adjectives.**

**1** I'm André. I live in France. I make pastries. They taste good and smell wonderful. I'm happy!

**2** I'm Alberto. I live in Costa Rica. I grow and sell flowers. I like my job. The flowers smell nice.

**3** I'm Candace. I live in Canada. I pick up rubbish in the city. The rubbish smells bad but I like my job.

**4** I'm Sarah. I live in Singapore. I work at a zoo. I take care of Zelda the elephant. Sometimes she smells awful.

**15** **Look at 14. Match and write.**

**1** André tastes

**2** Alberto smells

**3** Candace smells

**4** Sarah smells

**a** flowers. They smell _____.

**b** rubbish. It smells _____.

**c** Zelda the elephant. Zelda smells _____.

**d** pastries. They taste _____.

**16** **Do you like these jobs? Write numbers to rate them.**

1 = I love it!     2 = I like it.     3 = I don't like it.

_____ Pick up rubbish.

_____ Grow and sell flowers.

_____ Make pastries.

_____ Work at a zoo.

**17** **Read and circle T for true or F for false.**

1 A paragraph starts with a final sentence.     T    F

2 A topic sentence is the first sentence in a paragraph.     T    F

3 There are usually a few detail sentences in a paragraph.     T    F

4 A paragraph finishes with a title.     T    F

**18** **Read. Match the final sentence to each paragraph.**

1 My favourite animals are sea lions. They sound funny. They can do great tricks and can swim.

2 Butterflies are interesting. They look beautiful and they can fly. They taste with their legs!

3 My grandma's house smells good. Her cookies taste delicious. She plays the piano. The music sounds wonderful.

a They are my favourite insects!

b It's a great place to visit.

c They are wonderful animals.

**19** **Write a final sentence.**

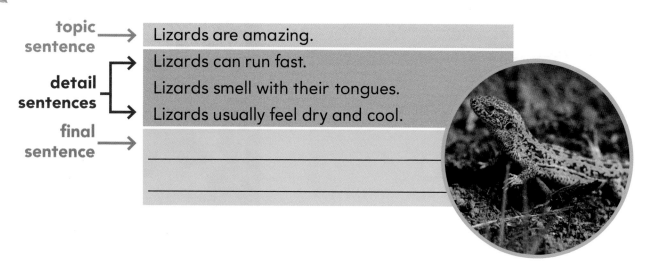

topic sentence → Lizards are amazing.

detail sentences →
Lizards can run fast.
Lizards smell with their tongues.
Lizards usually feel dry and cool.

final sentence → _____
_____

**20** **Read and circle fl, pl, gl and bl.**

play     swan            slim

flag          glad

flip-flops                block

glass       black

plum

**21** **Underline the words with fl, pl, gl and bl. Then read aloud.**

**1** There is a castle with a black flag.

**2** Drink the glass of orange juice and eat the plum cake.

**22** **Connect the letters. Then write.**

**1** fl          um          **a** _ _ _ _

**2** pl          ack         **b** _ _ _ _ _

**3** gl          ag          **c** _ _ _ _

**4** bl          ass         **d** _ _ _ _ _

2:52

**23** **Listen and write.**

It's summer.

Yellow ¹ _____,

Green ² _____.

³ _____,

⁴ _____ shorts,

It's summer.

I'm ⁵ _____!

**24** **Look and write.**

**1** It _____ delicious.

**2** They _____ good.

**3** It _____ hot.

**4** She _____ beautiful.

**5** They _____ loud.

**25** **Complete the questions and answer for you.**

**1** _____ your hair look today?

_____

**2** _____ new clothes feel?

_____

**3** _____ a butterfly look?

_____

**4** _____ your shoes feel?

_____

My hair looks bad today.

# Max's Day at the Zoo

**1** **Look at the paths for Max's day at the zoo. Complete the sentences. Use words from the boxes.**

| ANIMALS |
| --- |
| an owl |
| a shark |
| a camel |

| SENSES |
| --- |
| sounds |
| looks |
| tastes |
| feels |

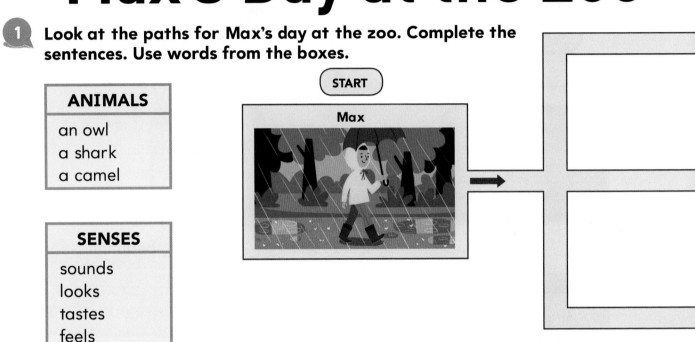

START

Max

**2** **Look at the paths again. What do you think? Write the answers.**

**1** Animal Quiz

It doesn't live in oceans.

It lives in deserts.

It can't fly but it can run fast.

What is it?

_____

**2** What was the weather like?

Before the zoo, _____ .

After the zoo, _____ .

**3** **Choose one path. Draw the path. Learn about Max's day at the zoo.**

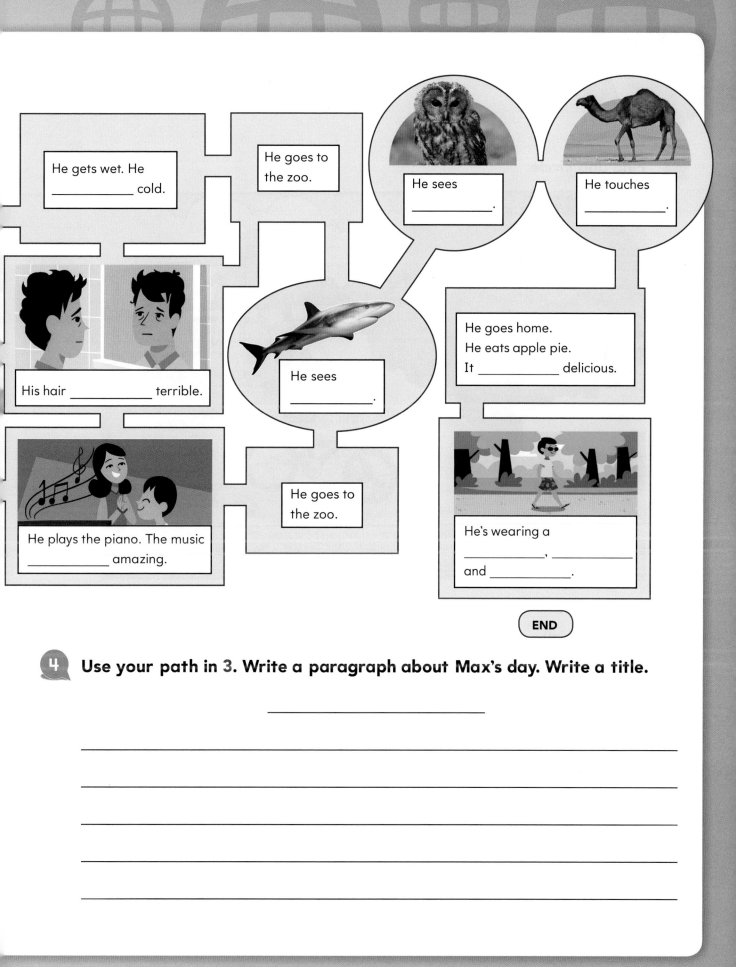

He gets wet. He _____ cold.

He goes to the zoo.

He sees _____.

He touches _____.

His hair _____ terrible.

He sees _____.

He goes home.
He eats apple pie.
It _____ delicious.

He plays the piano. The music _____ amazing.

He goes to the zoo.

He's wearing a _____, _____ and _____.

END

**4** **Use your path in 3. Write a paragraph about Max's day. Write a title.**

_____

_____

_____

_____

_____

_____

# unit 7 Fabulous Food!

**1** **Find and circle.**

| | | | |
|---|---|---|---|
| **1** bread | **2** cheese | **3** green pepper | **4** lettuce |
| **5** mushroom | **6** onions | **7** cucumbers | **8** pizza |
| **9** tomatoes | | | |

**2** **Draw your favourite food and write.**

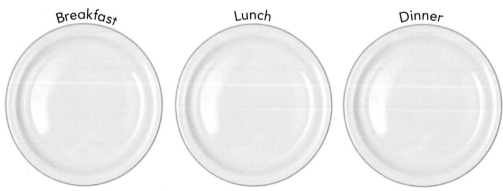

Breakfast      Lunch      Dinner

For breakfast, I like eating _____

_____.

**3:05**

**3** Listen and circle the five incorrect words. Then listen and write.

### I'm Hungry!

Hi, Mum, I'm home from school.
I'm really hungry now.
I'd like to make a burger,
Can you show me how?

**I am home from my school day.**
**I'd like a sandwich. Is that OK?**

Are there any onions?
Here are some on the shelf.
Is there any mustard?
I see it for myself.

**Chorus**

There's just one problem, Mum.
There isn't any lettuce!
But I've got a great idea:
Let's have cake instead!

**Chorus**

1 _____

2 _____

3 _____

4 _____

5 _____

**4** Find and write. Then complete for you.

1 reneg speerpp  2 zizap

_____ _____    _____

3 rushmooms  4 atootm cause

_____    _____ _____

I like _____ and _____.

I don't like _____ or _____.

Unit 7 **67**

**5** Read and write. Use the words in the box.

## A Surprise for Mum

Amy and Luke want to make dinner. It's a surprise for their mum. There's a green pepper, some cheese and some olives. The cheese and olives are yummy so Luke and Amy eat them. They take some more food out of the fridge. Mum comes home. The surprise isn't dinner. The surprise is a messy kitchen!

**1** Amy and Luke are making _____ for their mum.

**2** Amy and Luke eat the cheese and _____.

**3** Amy and Luke find some more _____ in the fridge.

**4** Their _____ isn't happy when she comes home.

**5** Mum's surprise is a _____ kitchen.

> dinner
> food
> messy
> mum
> olives

**6** Look at the story picture in 5. Read and circle the correct answer.

**1** Is there a pineapple on the table?　　**Yes, there is. / No, there isn't.**

**2** Are there any mushrooms?　　**Yes, there are. / No, there aren't.**

**3** Is there any cheese?　　**Yes, there is. / No, there isn't.**

**4** Are there any olives on the table?　　**Yes, there are. / No, there aren't.**

**THINK BIG** What do you need to make a cake? Find out and ✓.

eggs ☐　　butter ☐　cheese ☐　mushrooms ☐

sugar ☐　　flour ☐　onions ☐　strawberries ☐

**3:08**

**7** Listen and stick. Then listen and write the food.

1 _____

2 _____

3 _____

4 _____

**8** Look and circle.

1 There **are some / aren't any** mushrooms.

2 There **is some / isn't any** mustard.

3 There **is some / isn't any** bread.

4 There **are some / aren't any** cucumbers.

5 There **is some / isn't any** lettuce.

6 There **are some / aren't any** green peppers.

**9** **Look and answer. Use some or any.**

**1** Is there any milk? _____

**2** Is there any turkey? _____

**3** Is there any tomato sauce? _____

**4** Are there any eggs? _____

**5** Are there any red peppers? _____

**10** **Look at 9. Write the questions.**

**1** _____ Yes, there is some cheese.

**2** _____ Yes, there is some mustard.

**3** _____ No, there aren't any onions.

**4** _____ Yes, there are some green peppers.

**5** _____ No, there isn't any juice.

**11** **Read. Then write A, B, C, D or E.**

| | Where do we get the vitamins in food? |
|---|---|
| **Vitamin A** | carrots, mangoes, milk, eggs |
| **Vitamin B** | potatoes, bread, chicken, cheese, eggs, green vegetables |
| **Vitamin C** | oranges, peppers, tomatoes, potatoes |
| **Vitamin D** | eggs, fish, milk, the sun |
| **Vitamin E** | nuts, green vegetables |

**1** Vitamin ____   **2** Vitamin ____, ____ and ____   **3** Vitamin ____

**4** Vitamin ____   **5** Vitamin ____ and ____   **6** Vitamin ____

3:12

 **12** **Listen and circle.**

**1** Vitamin A is good for our **eyes** / **ears**.

**2** Vitamin B helps make blood and gives us **energy** / **skin**.

**3** Vitamin C is good for bones, teeth and our **brain** / **muscles**.

**4** Vitamin D helps makes strong **skin** / **bones**.

**5** Vitamin E keeps our **blood** / **muscles** healthy.

 **Write and draw.**

I get Vitamin ____ from

_____.

**13** **Read. Write the name of the person.**

    **Yoko** is from Japan. In the morning, she usually has rice, soup and fish.
**Luis** is from Spain. In the morning, he sometimes has churros – small doughnuts.
**Camila** is from Mexico. In the morning, she usually eats huevos rancheros.
**Tony** is from Australia. In the morning, he likes to eat toast with beans on top.

Mexico

huevos rancheros

1 _____

Australia

beans and toast

2 _____

Japan

rice, soup and fish

3 _____

Spain

churros

4 _____

**14** **Look at 13. What do you want to eat and why?**

I want to eat _____

_____.

title ⟶ **My Favourite Breakfast**
by Laura Brown

topic
sentence ⟶ I like a lot of different things for breakfast but I have my favourite breakfast every Sunday morning.

detail
sentences ⟶ I start with some orange slices, cold from the fridge. Then my mother makes two fluffy pancakes for me. I put butter on them and then I put warm maple syrup on top. The pancakes are delicious with a glass of cold milk.

final
sentence ⟶ My favourite breakfast makes Sundays special.

**15** **Write. Use the words in the box.**

> detail sentences    final sentence    title    topic sentence

1 _____ ⟶ Huevos rancheros are the best breakfast food.

2 _____ ⟶ Sunday Morning Breakfast with Huevos Rancheros

3 _____ ⟶ My mum starts with a tortilla. She toasts the tortilla in a pan and then puts the tortilla on a plate. I help her fry some eggs in a pan. Then she puts the eggs on top of the tortilla. I put salsa on the eggs and they taste amazing!

4 _____ ⟶ My mum makes huevos rancheros for breakfast on Sunday mornings.

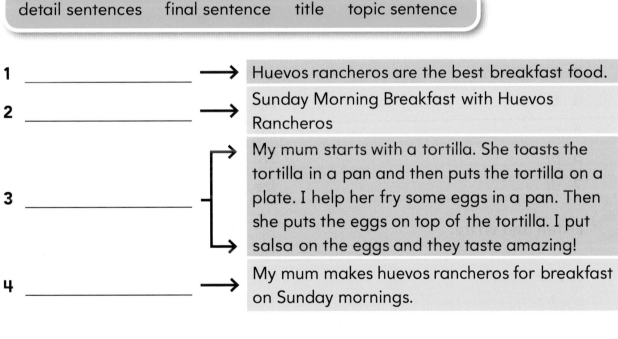

**16** **Look at 15. Write the paragraph in order.**

_____

_____

_____

_____

_____

**17** **Read and circle br, cr, dr, fr, gr, pr and tr.**

bread    grass    dream    glad

cream    frog    prize    train

plant

**18** **Underline the words with br, cr, dr, fr, gr, pr and tr. Then read aloud.**

**1** The frog's driving the green and brown train.

**2** She's crying because she's got a prize and she's happy.

**19** **Connect the letters. Then write.**

**1** br          eam     **a** _ _ _ _ _
**2** cr          oll     **b** _ _ _ _ _
**3** fr          ead     **c** _ _ _ _ _
**4** tr          ass     **d** _ _ _ _ _
**5** gr          og      **e** _ _ _ _
**6** pr          ive     **f** _ _ _ _ _
**7** dr          ize     **g** _ _ _ _ _

3:19

**20** **Listen and write.**

Every night,
I ¹_____
About a ²_____
And a ³_____
And a ⁴_____
⁵_____!
In my dream,
They eat ⁶_____
With ⁷_____.

**21** **Look. Then circle the different kinds of food.**

**1**

**The sandwich has got:**

| | |
|---|---|
| bread | green peppers |
| tomatoes | mustard |
| turkey | onions |
| cheese | lettuce |

**2**

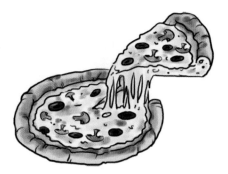

**The pizza has got:**

| | |
|---|---|
| mustard | lettuce |
| cheese | olives |
| tomato sauce | ice cream |
| chicken | mushrooms |

**3**

**The salad has got:**

| | |
|---|---|
| tomato sauce | cucumbers |
| turkey | milk |
| lettuce | cheese |
| onions | chicken |
| green peppers | tomatoes |

**22** **Look at 21 and answer.**

**1** Is there any lettuce in the sandwich? _____

**2** Is there any mustard on the pizza? _____

**3** Are there any olives on the pizza? _____

**4** Are there any onions in the salad? _____

**23** **Write about your home.**

**1** Are there any tomatoes in your fridge? _____

**2** Is there any milk in your fridge? _____

# unit 8 Healthy Living

**1** Write. Use activities from the box. Then ✓ the healthy ones.

| | | |
|---|---|---|
| drank lots of water | got two hours of sleep | ate pie for breakfast |
| rode a bike | ate a healthy breakfast | got ten hours of sleep |

1 _____
_____ ☐

2 _____
_____ ☐

3 _____
_____ ☐

4 _____
_____ ☐

5 _____
_____ ☐

6 _____
_____ ☐

**2** Read and circle for you.

1 How do you feel today? I feel **great** / **awful** / **OK** today.

2 Did you get enough sleep? **Yes** / **No**

3 Did you eat any breakfast? **Yes** / **No**

4 Did you drink lots of water? **Yes** / **No**

5 Did you ride your bike? **Yes** / **No**

6 Did you have a healthy lunch? **Yes** / **No**

7 Did you do any exercise? **Yes** / **No**

**3** **Listen and write.**

| any | Did | enough | good | too | you |

## Live Right!

Did you eat breakfast? asks Mum,
You don't look ¹_____ to me.
Did you get ²_____ sleep? asks Mum,
Did you watch ³_____much TV?

**Enough sleep. Good food.
Be healthy. Live right!
Enough sleep. Good food.
Be healthy. Live right!**

⁴_____ you ride your bike? asks Mum,
You know it's good for ⁵_____.
Did you get ⁶_____ exercise?
You know it's good to do!

***Chorus***

**4** **Read and ✓ for you. Then answer with Yes, I did or No, I didn't.**

| My Habits Last Week | Sun | Mon | Tue | Wed | Thu | Fri | Sat |
|---|---|---|---|---|---|---|---|
| **1** got enough sleep | | | | | | | |
| **2** drank enough water | | | | | | | |
| **3** ate healthy food | | | | | | | |

Did you get enough sleep?  _____

Did you drink enough water?  _____

Did you eat enough healthy food?  _____

**5** **Read and answer. Write Yes, she did or No, she didn't.**

### An Unhealthy Dinner

Amy's dad wants her to be healthy. Amy likes unhealthy food. She ate burger and chips for her dinner. Fried food isn't healthy. She drank a large cola. Cola isn't healthy. It's got lots of sugar. Now, Amy doesn't feel very well.

**1** Did Amy eat burger and chips for dinner? _____

**2** Did she eat fried food? _____

**3** Did she drink a large glass of water? _____

**4** Did she eat a healthy dinner? _____

**6** **What did you eat for dinner yesterday? Was it healthy? Draw, write and circle.**

Yesterday for dinner, I ate _____

and I drank _____.

My dinner **was / wasn't** healthy.

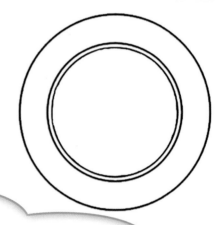

**Healthy or unhealthy? Draw.**

**THINK BIG**

chips    lettuce    tomatoes    bottle of cola    burger    water

3:27

**7** Listen and stick. What did Grace and Carlos do at the weekend?

Sunday

1 _____

Saturday

2 _____

Sunday

3 _____

**8** Read and complete with **did** or **didn't**.

1 **Lou:** Are you feeling OK?

**Jack:** I'm tired.

**Lou:** _____ you exercise today?

**Jack:** No, I _____. I played video games all day.

**Lou:** Oh. _____ you sleep eight hours?

**Jack:** No, I _____. I slept four hours.

2 **Ellen:** Hi, Jim. I feel great today! How are you?

**Jim:** Not good. I _____ eat a good breakfast.

**Ellen:** What _____ you eat?

**Jim:** I ate ice cream and I drank cola.

**Ellen:** Really? What _____ you eat for lunch?

**Jim:** I forgot lunch. I _____ eat lunch.

**9** **Look and circle.**

| Yesterday Morning | Yesterday Afternoon | Yesterday Evening |

**1** They **ate dinner** / **woke up** yesterday evening.

**2** They **watched TV** / **woke up** yesterday afternoon.

**3** They **ate dinner** / **woke up** yesterday morning.

**10** **Look and answer.**

**1** Did he get enough sleep?  _____

**2** Did she get enough sleep?  _____

**3** Did they get enough exercise?  _____

**4** Did she eat a healthy dinner?  _____

**5** Did he eat a healthy dinner?  _____

**6** Did she drink any water?  _____

**7** Did he drink enough water?  _____

**11** **Read and complete. Use the words in the box.**

| active | activities | energy | measure | put on weight | watching TV |

A calorie is a ¹_____ of the energy we get from food. We need calories to give us ²_____ to do different activities and sports. Some ³_____, such as riding a bike and dancing, use a lot of calories and are really good for us. Sleeping and ⁴_____ don't use any calories. If we eat more calories than we use, we can ⁵_____ so it's important to stay ⁶_____.

**12** **Complete the diagram. Add five more activities.**

| dancing   doing gymnastics   playing basketball   playing video games   playing tennis   riding a bike   running   sleeping   watching a DVD |

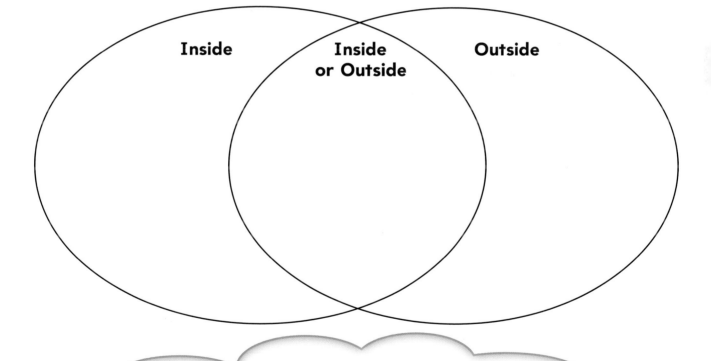

**Inside**       **Inside or Outside**       **Outside**

**THINK BIG** **Find out and circle which activities are good for your body.**

1 Sleeping for **eight** / **twelve** hours a day.

2 Playing **six hours** / **one hour** of football a day.

3 Eating a **big** / **small** breakfast.

**13** **Read and match. Then write.**

**a**

Footvolley

**b**

Octopush

**c**

Pumpkin Regatta

**1** In some parts of the United States and Canada, people play this sport. The people sit in pumpkins and they race. This sport is called _____.

**2** People play this sport all over the world. It is like hockey but players play it in water. Players use a small stick. They try to push a ball into a net. This sport is called _____.

**3** People play this sport in Brazil. They play it on the beach. They cannot touch the ball with their hands. This sport is called _____.

**14** **Read and match.**

**1** Octopush is like hockey

**2** A pumpkin regatta is like a boat race

**3** Footvolley is like volleyball

**a** but people do not race in boats.

**b** but the players use a football.

**c** but people play it in water.

**15** **Make up a strange sport. Draw and describe it.**

The sport is called _____

_____

_____

_____

_____

**16** **Read and circle.**

1 I usually walk to school **or** / **but** today I rode my bike.

2 I sometimes play tennis **and** / **but** baseball after school.

3 I can walk to school **or** / **but** I can take a bus to school.

4 I like dancing **and** / **but** I'm not very good at it.

5 I usually get eight **and** / **or** nine hours of sleep.

6 It's hot **but** / **and** sunny today.

**17** **Read and write. Use the ideas in the box.**

> and I help her do the dishes
> but he isn't good at basketball
> but she sounds terrible
> or I take the bus

1 My friend always plays the guitar _____.

2 My brother is good at flying kites _____.

3 My dad drives me to school _____.

4 I help my mum cook dinner _____.

**18** **Read and complete with or, but or and.**

I think I live a healthy life. I love doing exercise ¹_____
playing sports. I usually play tennis ²_____ volleyball
on Saturday ³_____ when it's rainy I go running inside
in a gym. I sometimes have a burger ⁴_____ chips for
lunch ⁵_____ I usually eat turkey and rice
⁶_____ pizza and salad.

**19** **Read and circle all, au and aw.**

ball

haul

cry

yawn

draw

tall

prince

claw

**20** **Underline the words with all, au and aw. Then read aloud.**

**1** Paul, don't kick the ball to the wall.

**2** Draw a tiger with big claws.

**21** **Connect the letters. Then write.**

**1** sm          aul          **a** _ _ _ _

**2** dr           all          **b** _ _ _ _ _

**3** h            aw           **c** _ _ _ _

3:36

**22** **Listen and write.**

I'm ¹ _____, I'm bored.

Yawn, ² _____ .

Let's play, let's play

With a ³ _____,

Let's ⁴ _____,

Let's draw a ⁵ _____ .

**23** **Circle the correct verb.**

1 Did they **eat** / **ate** a healthy lunch?

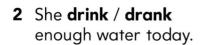

2 She **drink** / **drank** enough water today.

3 She didn't **play** / **played** volleyball today.

**24** **Read and complete. Use the words in the box.**

> any   didn't   enough   got   healthy   rode

1 John didn't get _____ sleep last night. He woke up at 4 a.m.

2 John _____ eat breakfast this morning.

3 John didn't get _____ exercise today. He watched TV all day.

4 Sue _____ enough sleep last night.

5 Sue ate a _____ breakfast this morning.

6 Sue _____ her bike to school today.

**25** **Complete the sentences. Use the words.**

1 _____ football is good fun and it's good for my health. (play)

2 _____ is good for your body. (run)

3 _____ my bike is good for my health. (ride)

4 _____ is important. But don't sleep too much! (sleep)

5 _____ turkey and rice is good for me. (eat)

# unit 9 School Trips!

 **1** **Look and write.**

aquarium    art gallery    dairy farm    museum    national park    zoo

**1** _____

**2** _____

**3** _____

**4** _____

**5** _____

**6** _____

**2** **Look, read and circle. Then number.**

**1** We went to a national park. We learned about
   **a** penguins.          **b** rocks.          **c** music.

**2** We went to the zoo. We saw
   **a** dinosaurs.          **b** elephants.          **c** paintings.

**3** We went to a dairy farm. We learned about
   **a** rocks.          **b** paintings.          **c** cows.

**4** We went to a concert hall. We heard
   **a** some music.          **b** sea lions.          **c** some cows.

**3** **Listen and number in order.**

## Learning Out of School

Where did you go?
What did you see?
We went to the zoo, we saw a play,
We had a great time!

I like going on school trips
Learning out of school.
We go to lots of places.
They're interesting and cool!

**School trips. School trips.**
**They're a lot of fun.**
**School trips. School trips.**
**Let's go on one!**

Aquarium, theatre, concert hall and zoo,
We saw some great things.
There was lots to do!

**Chorus**

**4** **Write.**

My favourite school trip is _____.

**5** **Read and write.**

| art gallery | concert hall | dairy farm | theatre | zoo |

**1** I didn't see any giraffes but I saw a hippo and zebra.
_____

**2** I learned about French artists. _____

**3** I saw a play about animals. _____

**4** We saw about five hundred cows! They were
smelly. _____

**5** There were drums, violins and guitars there and the
music was great. _____

**6** **Read. Then write Luke or Amy.**

**A Cool Trip**

Luke and Amy went on a trip. They went to the Red Rock National Park. They learned about many kinds of rocks. Amy liked the trip a lot. Luke didn't like the trip. He didn't like the rocks and he didn't like walking. Amy got a present for Luke. It was a rock!

**1** _____ really liked the trip.

**2** _____ didn't like the trip.

**3** _____ didn't like the rocks.

**4** _____ got a present for her brother.

**7** **Imagine a school trip. Then answer.**

**1** Where did you go?

_____

**2** When did you go?

_____

**3** What did you see?

_____

**4** Did you like the trip?

_____

**What happens next in the story? Write.**

**THINK BIG**

_____

_____

_____

3:44

**8** **Listen and stick.**

a

b

c

d
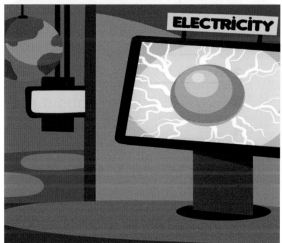

**9** **Write. Complete the dialogue.**

**A:** Where ¹_____ you go on your school trip?

**B:** We ²_____ to a dairy farm.

**A:** What ³_____ you see?

**B:** We saw farmers milk cows.

**A:** Did you ⁴_____ it?

**B:** No, I ⁵_____.
The cows smelled awful!

**10** **Think about a trip you took. Draw and answer.**

Where did you go?

**You:** _____

What did you see?

**You:** _____

What did you do?

**You:** _____

**11** **Complete. Then match.**

heard   learned   saw (x2)

1 _____ a film about dinosaurs        **a** national park

2 _____ a play about animals          **b** concert hall

3 _____ about rocks and nature        **c** museum

4 _____ some music                     **d** theatre

**12** **Read and match. Make questions.**

**1** What       **a** did they go?

**2** Did        **b** did they see?

**3** Where      **c** they like it?

**13** **Look at 12. Write the questions. Imagine the answers.**

**1 A:** _____

   **B:** _____

**2 A:** _____

   **B:** _____

**3 A:** _____

   **B:** _____

**14** **Read and number.**

1  *Old Man with his Head in his Hands* is a painting by Vincent Van Gogh. Is it scary? Some people think so.

2  *The Little Giants* is a painting by Francisco de Goya. Many people think it's beautiful.

3  *Haystacks at Giverny* is by Claude Monet, a famous French artist. Some people say it's colourful but boring.

4  *Nature and Fantasy* is a painting by Giuseppe Arcimboldo. How many flowers can you see? Do you think it's colourful but strange?

a   b   c 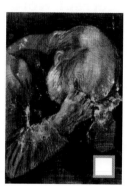  d

**15** **Look at the paintings in 14. Answer.**

1  Claude Monet loved painting near his home in France. Do you love a place? Where is it? _____

2  In *The Little Giants* there are some boys. They look happy. What makes you happy? _____

3  *Old Man with his Head in his Hands* is a painting of a scary-looking man. Think of something scary. What is it?

_____

**THINK BIG**  Find out about a famous painter. Find out his/her name, what he/she liked to paint and an interesting fact.

**16** Look and circle the correct word.

**1** Flamenco is a

    **a** puppet show.     **b** play.     **c** dance.

**2** Flamenco is from

    **a** England.     **b** Spain.     **c** Vietnam.

**3** Mua Roi Nuoc has got

    **a** actors.     **b** puppets.     **c** dancers.

**4** Mua Roi Nuoc is from

    **a** England.     **b** Spain.     **c** Vietnam.

**5** Shakespeare wrote plays in

    **a** Vietnam.     **b** Spain.     **c** England.

**6** Shakespeare's first name was

    **a** William.     **b** Romeo.     **c** Tony.

**17** Write and (✓).

My favourite story is _____.

I want to see my story

    ☐ in a dance.

    ☐ in a puppet show.

    ☐ in a play.

**18** **Underline subjects in red, verbs in blue and objects in purple.**

   **1** Sally and Craig went to the zoo.

   **2** I didn't see a sea lion show.

   **3** My parents went out for dinner.

   **4** We visited an art gallery.

   **5** Did you see any rocks?

**19** **What's missing? Write S for subject, V for verb and O for object. Then look and complete.**

> I   learned   like   paintings   they

   **1** They saw lots of _____.   ☐

   **2** We didn't _____ the play.   ☐

   **3** _____ watched a film today.   ☐

   **4** Ali and Peter _____ about dinosaurs.   ☐

   **5** Did _____ like it?   ☐

**20** **Put the paragraph in order. Now write your own.**

In my school, we go on school trips every month.

I want to go again. It was great fun!

A Trip to the Aquarium ☐

First, we saw penguins and turtles. Then we saw lots of sharks. These were my favourite. There was a whale show and it was amazing. I took some photos and we loved it.

_____

_____

_____

_____

_____

**21** **Read and circle nt, ld, nd and st.**

plant
ant
hand
call
nest
child
cold
draw
fast
band

**22** **Underline the words with nt, ld, nd and st. Then read aloud.**

**1** Put your hands in your pockets. It's cold.

**2** This is an ant's nest.

**23** **Connect the letters. Then write.**

**1** pla          ld     **a** _ _ _ _

**2** co           nd     **b** _ _ _ _

**3** ha           st     **c** _ _ _ _

**4** ne           nt     **d** _ _ _ _ _

3:54

**23** **Listen and write.**

An ¹ _____,
² _____
³ _____ playing
In the ⁴ _____.
A ⁵ _____
⁶ _____ playing in
A ⁷ _____.

**25** **Read the clues and write the places.**

1 The paintings were beautiful here.

   _____

2 I learned about penguins and zebras.

   _____

3 The music sounds amazing.

   _____

4 We saw sea lions and sharks.

   _____

**26** **Find the five adjectives. Use them to make sentences.**

avuwfunnysfionboringjomsinterestingzicqscaryeapostrangetyur

1 I think _____ **is / are** _____ because _____

   _____ .

2 I think _____ .

3 I _____ .

4 _____

5 _____

**27** **Complete the dialogues.**

1 **A:** My parents [1]_____ to a play last night. (go)

  **B:** [2]_____ they like it? (do)

  **A:** Yes, they [3]_____! (do)

  **B:** [4]_____ you in the play? (be)

  **A:** Yes, I [5]_____! (be)

2 **A:** Where [1]_____ you yesterday? (be)

  **B:** We [2]_____ to the museum. (go)

  **A:** Did you [3]_____ fun? (have)

  **B:** No, we [4]_____. (do not) We [5]_____ it. (not like)

Unit 9 **95**

# Matt's Day

**1** Look at the paths for Matt's day and complete the faces.

= healthy     = unhealthy

**2** Choose one path. Draw the path. Learn about Matt's day.

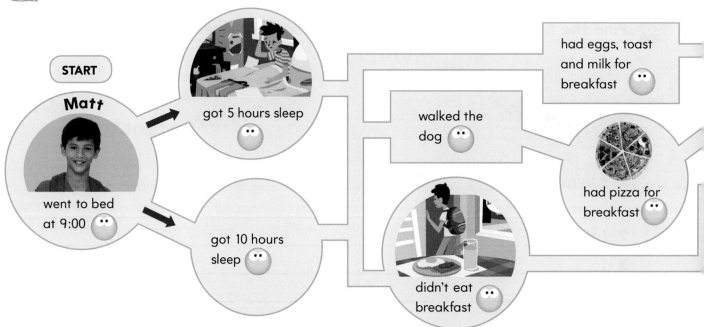

**3** Look at your path in 2. What do you think? Write the answers.

1  What time did Matt wake up? _____

2  Did Matt get enough sleep? _____

3  Did Matt get enough exercise? _____

4  Did Matt eat healthy food? _____

5  Where did Matt go on the school trip? What did he do? _____

_____

6  How did Matt feel in the evening? _____

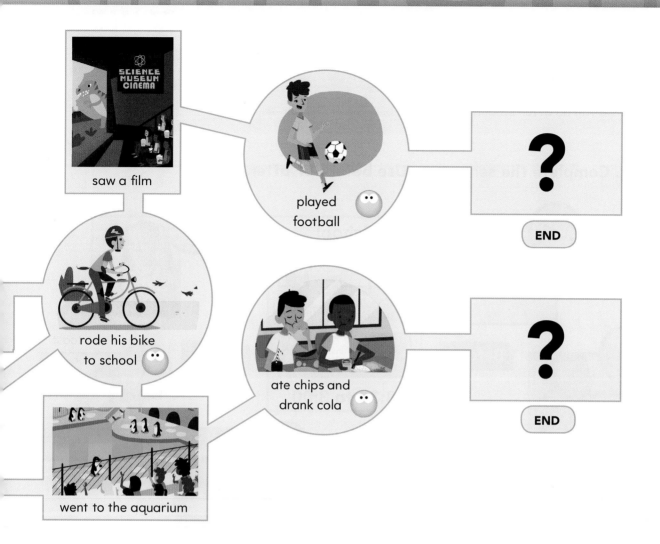

saw a film

played football

rode his bike to school

went to the aquarium

ate chips and drank cola

?

END

?

END

**4** **Use your path in 2. Write a paragraph about Matt's day. Write a title.**

_____

_____

_____

_____

_____

_____

_____

_____

_____

| What does he/she do **before** school? | He/She eats breakfast **before** school. |
|---|---|
| What do you do **after** school? | I play football **after** school. |

**1** **Look. Complete the sentences. Use before or after.**

Before

After

School

8:30 to 3:00

**1** She plays video games
_____ school.

**2** What does she do _____
school? She wakes up.

**3** She always gets dressed
_____ school.

**4** What does he have _____
school? He has cereal.

**5** He always watches TV
_____ school.

**6** What does she do _____
school? She does her homework.

**2** **Write about your family.**

**1** What does your mother do in the morning? _____

**2** What does your father do in the evening? _____

| | |
|---|---|
| **What does** he/she **do**? | He/She **is** a nurse. |
| **Where does** he/she **work**? | He/She **works** at a hospital. |
| **What do** your sisters **do**? | They**'re** (They **are**) nurses. |

**1** Look. Circle and complete the dialogues.

| Pete | Uncle – waiter | Dad – firefighter | Mum – cashier | | Katrina | cousin – student | cousin – student |

**1** **Katrina:** What **do / does** your father do?

**Pete:** He's a _____.

**Katrina:** Where **do / does** he work?

**Pete:** He **work / works** at a fire station.

**2** **Pete:** What **do / does** your cousins do?

**Katrina:** They are _____.

**Pete:** Where **do / does** they study?

**Katrina:** They **study / studies** at a university.

**3** **Katrina:** _____

**Pete:** He's a waiter.

**Katrina:** _____

**Pete:** He _____ at a restaurant.

**4** **Katrina:** _____

**Pete:** She's a cashier.

**Katrina:** _____

**Pete:** She works at a supermarket.

| What **does** he/she **have to** do? | He/She **has to** feed the fish. |
|---|---|
| What **do** you/we/they **have to** do? | I/We/You/They **have to** feed the fish. |

**1** **Look. Complete the questions and answers.**

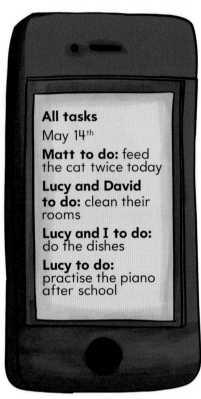

**All tasks**
May 14th
**Matt to do:** feed the cat twice today
**Lucy and David to do:** clean their rooms
**Lucy and I to do:** do the dishes
**Lucy to do:** practise the piano after school

**1 A:** What does Matt have to do?

   **B:** He _____.

**2 A:** What do Lucy and David have to do?

   **B:** They _____.

**3 A:** What _____ Lucy and I _____?

   **B:** You _____.

**4 A:** What _____ Lucy _____?

   **B:** She _____.

| I/You/We/They | **always** **usually** | do the dishes. |
|---|---|---|
| He/She | **sometimes** **never** | takes out the rubbish. |

**2** **Look. Write never, usually or always.**

| Everyday Habits | Mon | Tues | Wed | Thurs | Fri |
|---|---|---|---|---|---|
| **1** We _____ eat a good breakfast. | ✓ | ✓ | ✓ | ✓ | ✓ |
| **2** She _____ plays tennis after school. | | | | | |
| **3** I _____ wake up late. | ✓ | ✓ | ✓ | ✓ | |

| What **can** a penguin do? | It **can** swim. It **can't** fly. | subject + *can/can't* + verb |
| What **can** bears do? | They **can** climb. They **can't** fly. | |
| **Can** a penguin swim? | Yes, it **can**. | subject + *can/can't* |
| **Can** bears fly? | No, they **can't**. | |

**1** Write one animal name in each box in the chart.

a bear    a camel    lizards    penguins    sea lions    a snake

| What Can They Do? | Can | Can't |
| --- | --- | --- |
| **1** live in ice and snow | | |
| **2** do tricks | | |
| **3** live in deserts | | |

**2** Look at 1. Complete the dialogues.

**1  A:** _____ a penguin _____ in ice and snow?

**B:** Yes, _____ but a camel _____.

**3  A:** What _____ a camel _____?

**B:** _____ live in deserts.

**5  A:** _____ a bear live in forests?

**B:** _____.

**2  A:** What can lizards do?

**B:** They _____ live in deserts.

**4  A:** Can a bear live in deserts?

**B:** No, it _____.

**6  A:** What _____ sea lions _____?

**B:** Sea lions _____ tricks but they _____ talk.

| What **is** the weather like today? | It**'s** hot and sunny. |
|---|---|
| What **was** the weather **like** yesterday? | It **was** sunny. We **were** warm. |

**1** Look. Complete the questions and answers.

**Carla**

**Massi**

**Yoko**

| Barcelona, Spain | |
|---|---|
| Yesterday | Today |
| 32°C | 32°C |

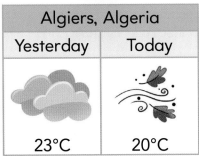

| Algiers, Algeria | |
|---|---|
| Yesterday | Today |
| 23°C | 20°C |

| Sapporo, Japan | |
|---|---|
| Yesterday | Today |
| 10°C | 5°C |

**1 Massi:** What _____ the weather like today in Barcelona?

   **Carla:** It _____ hot and rainy.

**2 Yoko:** What _____ the weather like yesterday in Algiers?

   **Massi:** It _____ warm and cloudy.

**3 Carla:** _____ today in Sapporo?

   **Yoko:** _____

**2** Look at **1**. Complete the dialogues.

**1 A:** _____

   **B:** It was hot and sunny.

**2 A:** What is the weather like today in Algiers?

   **B:** _____

**3 A:** What was the weather like in Sapporo yesterday?

   **B:** _____

| How **does** the apple pie **taste**? | It **tastes** delicious. |
|---|---|
| How **do** your new shoes **feel**? | They **feel** good. |

**1** **Look. Match the words and write the sentences.**

**1**  **2**  **3**  **4**

| **1** | The flowers | looks | awful. | _____ |
| **2** | The cheese | smell | tight. | _____ |
| **3** | The shoes | look | nice. | _____ |
| **4** | The shirt | smells | comfortable. | _____ |

**2** **Write the questions.**

**1 A:** _____

**B:** The music sounds nice.

**2 A:** _____

**B:** The cookies taste delicious.

**3 A:** _____

**B:** The scarf feels soft.

**4 A:** _____

**B:** The perfume smells nice.

| | | | |
|---|---|---|---|
| Is there **any** pizza? | Yes, there is **some** pizza. | Are there **any** onions? | Yes, there are **some** onions. |
| Is there **any** fish? | No, there isn't **any** fish. | Are there **any** eggs? | No, there aren't **any** eggs. |

**1** **Look and write.**

lettuce
mustard
bread
cucumber

**2** **Look at 1. Write some or any.**

**1** There is _____ lettuce.

**2** There isn't _____ tomato sauce.

**3** There aren't _____ tomatoes.

**4** There are _____ cucumbers.

**3** **Write questions and answers. Then draw the sandwich.**

**1** Are there _____ bananas?

Yes, there are _____ bananas.

**2** _____ onions?

No, there aren't _____ onions.

**3** _____ yoghurt?

_____ yoghurt.

**4** _____ chips?

_____ chips.

Silly Sandwich

| **Did** you/he/she/they **get** enough sleep yesterday? | Yes, I/he/she/they **did**. | No, I/he/she/they **didn't**. |
| --- | --- | --- |

**1** **Read and match.**

1 Did you have      **a** to the zoo?

2 Did they eat      **b** Sue ride their bikes?

3 Did she go      **c** you see any rocks?

4 Did he      **d** a healthy lunch?

5 Did      **e** visit a museum?

6 Did Al and      **f** fun?

**2** **Look. Write questions and answers.**

**1** **A:** Did Matt eat any breakfast?

    **B:** No, _____.

**2** **A:** _____ enough sleep?

    **B:** No, _____.

**3** **A:** Did Sue have a big breakfast?

    **B:** Yes, _____.

**4** **A:** _____ some exercise?

    **B:** Yes, _____.

| Where **did** you/he/she/they **go**? | I/He/She/They **went** to the Science Museum. | |
| --- | --- | --- |
| What **did** you/he/she/they **see**? | I/He/She/They **saw** an interesting film about dinosaurs. | |
| **Did** you/he/she/they **like** it? | Yes, I/he/she/they **liked** it. | No, I /he/she/they **didn't like** it. |

**1** **Find and circle the past form of the verbs. Then match.**

| l | g | r | d | r | a | n | k | z | **1** eat |
| a | t | e | m | z | m | l | k | o | **2** do |
| p | o | n | h | a | d | x | u | i | **3** drink |
| i | n | e | h | r | g | d | i | d | **4** get |
| a | f | g | c | g | o | t | s | w | **5** have |
| z | x | c | v | b | r | o | d | e | **6** ride |

**2** **Look and circle. Then answer.**

Jeff and Jack

Tim

**1** Where did Jeff and Jack **go / went** yesterday?  _____

**2** What did they **see / saw**?  _____

**3** Where **does / did** Tim go last weekend?  _____

**4** **Does / Did** Tim like it?  _____

# Young Learners English Practice Movers: Listening A

## – 5 questions –

 **Look at the picture. Listen and look. There is one example.**

Mary          John          Vicky          Fred

Jack          Sally

# Young Learners English Practice Movers: Listening B

## – 5 questions –

**Look at the pictures. Now listen and look. There is one example.**

What is his job?

**A** ☐

**B** ✔

**C** ☐

**1**  What is her job?

**A** ☐

**B** ☐

**C** ☐

**2**  What time does she usually stop working?

**A** ☐

**B** ☐

**C** ☐

# Young Learners English Practice Movers: Listening B

**3** What does she have to do every day?

A

B

C

**4** What does she like about her job?

A

B

C

**5** What job would she like to have in the future?

A

B

C

# Young Learners English Practice Movers: Listening C

 **Listen and look. There is one example.**

Susie's School Trip

What Susie did today: _____ *went on a school trip* _____

**1** Where she went: _____

**2** What she did in the morning: _____

**3** What she had for lunch: _____

**4** What she did in the afternoon: _____

**5** What she learned: _____

# Young Learners English Practice Movers: Reading & Writing A

**Read the text. Choose the correct words and write them on the lines.**

**Example** Bears live in many different kinds of places around the _____world_____. Some bears live in forests and mountains. Grizzly bears, for example, live in the Rocky Mountains, in the United States.

1 They explore when the _____ is warm and they sleep during the long

2 winter. They _____ climb trees and catch fish.

Polar bears live in the Arctic, where it's

3 _____ and cold all year round.

4 They've got thick _____ to protect them from the cold and they

5 hunt for fish under the _____. Like all other bears, they fit right into their environment.

**Example** ocean  desert  world

1 weather  water  world

2 can  should  will

3 snowy  hot  rainy

4 feathers  beaks  fur

5 rock  ice  wood

# Young Learners English Practice Movers: Reading & Writing B

**– 6 questions –**

**Read the story. Choose a word from the box. Write the correct word next to numbers 1–6. There is one example.**

Today starts off like any other day for Paul. He _____*wakes up*_____ and

gets out of bed. Then he goes into the bathroom and

1_____. After that, he 2_____

and takes the bus to school. But something is different today. At lunch, he

doesn't have to wait in line. The other kids let him go to the front. After

school, Paul comes home. He usually has to 3_____ and

take him for a walk but today his sister does it for him. In the evening, Paul's

mum cooks his favourite dinner. He always has to 4_____

after dinner but today he gets a break. Instead of doing chores, he gets to

5_____ with his brother and sister. What's different about

today? It's Paul's birthday. He almost always 6_____ at

8 o'clock but today his parents let him stay up late and eat ice cream.

"I wish every day was like today," says Paul.

**example**

wakes up

eats breakfast

play football

do the dishes

does homework

goes to bed

washes his face

feed the dog

play games

**(7) Now choose the best name for the story.**

**Tick (✔) one box.**

My Everyday Life ☐

A Very Special Day ☐

Time for a Break ☐

# Young Learners English Practice Movers: Reading & Writing C

**Look and read. Write yes or no.**

**Examples**

It's cold and windy today.                                     _____no_____

People are watching a play.                               _____yes_____

**Questions**

1 A woman is jogging. _____

2 A family are having a picnic. _____

3 There are some sandwiches on a plate. _____

4 A girl is walking her dog. _____

5 People are watching a film. _____

6 There is some lemonade for sale. _____

   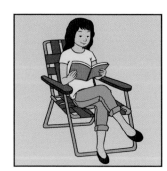

# Young Learners English Practice Movers: Speaking B

# Wordlist

ask a question with:

**What time...**

ask a question with:

**When...**

ask a question with:

**in the morning / afternoon / evening**

ask a question with:

**at _____:_____ (time)**

ask a question with:

**before work**

ask a question with:

**after work**

answer with:

**I...**

answer with:

**I always...**

answer with:

**I usually...**

answer with:

**I sometimes...**

answer with:

**I never...**

answer with:

**I have to...**

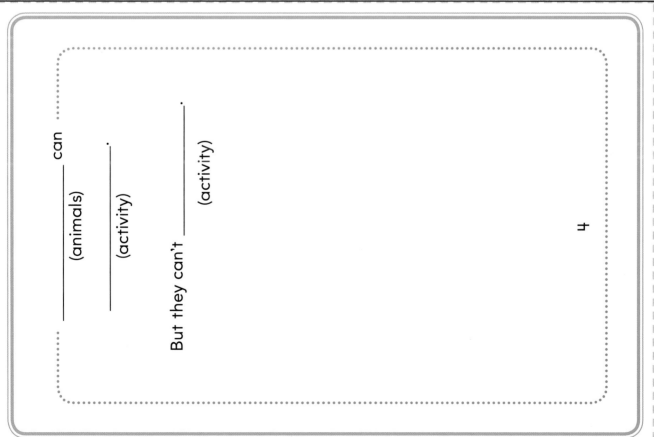

**All About** _____
(animals)

© 2014 Pearson Education, Inc.

_____ can ..........
(animals)

_____ .
(activity)

But they can't _____ .
(activity)

4

**2**

_____ live in

(animals)

_____ .

(habitat)

It's _____ there.

(weather word)

**3**

_____ eat

(animals)

_____ .

(food)

**Dialogue 2**

A: Did you eat breakfast this morning?

B: Yes, it was awesome. Sharks are cool!

A: Did you like it?

B: I ate turkey and lettuce.

A: What did you do there?

B: Yes, I had eggs on toast. I'm ready for the baseball game!!

A: What did you eat for dinner?

B: We went to the aquarium.

A: Where did you go yesterday?

B: We saw a film about sharks.

# My BIG ENGLISH World

## 3

My name: _____
My age: _____
My address: _____

My family: _____

ME

FOLD

©2014 Pearson Education, Ltd.

# ENGLISH
## AROUND ME

Look around you. Paste or draw things with English words. Write everyday words.

Everyday Words

FILM TICKET

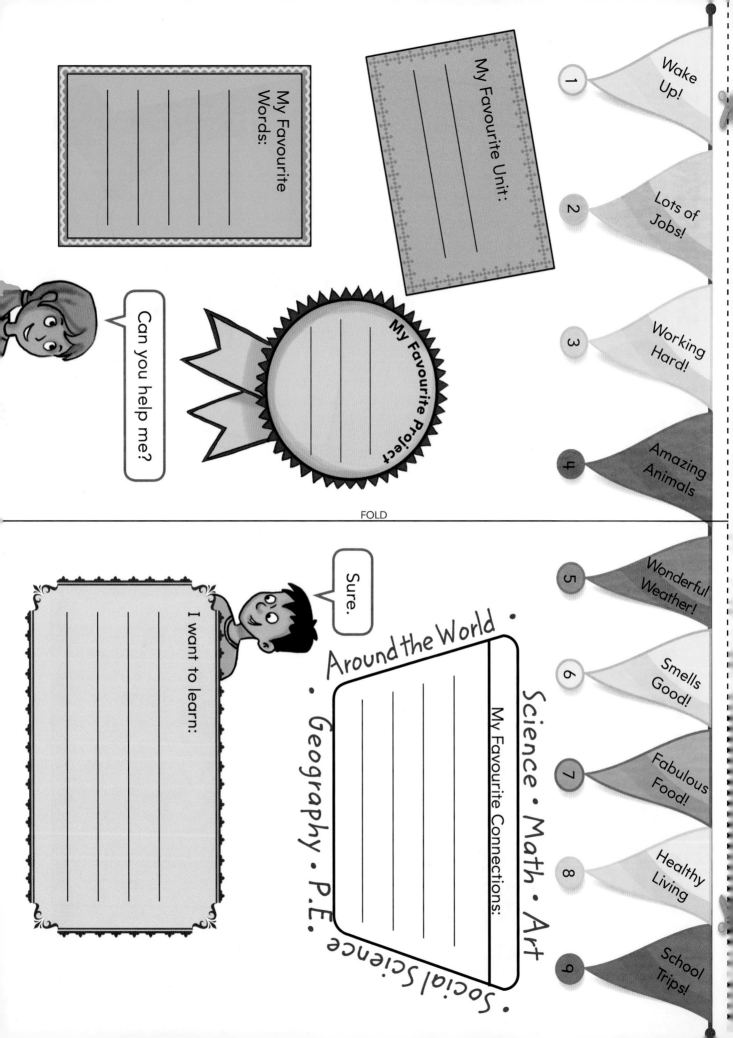

## 4

**Unit 1, page 9**

**Unit 2, page 19**

**Unit 3, page 29**

**Unit 4, page 41**

## Unit 5, page 51

## Unit 6, page 61

**Unit 7, page 73**

**Unit 8, page 83**

**Unit 9, page 93**